Famous Florida Recipes

Recipes

300 Years Of Good Eating

by LOWIS CARLTON

Formerly Food Editor, *The Miami Herald*
Food columnist, Florida Dept. of Agriculture
Food Editor, *Palm Beach Life Magazine*

Illustrations by Joseph Brown, Jr.

Copyright © 1972 by Lowis Carlton
All Rights Reserved

ISBN: 0-8200-0804-4
LC No.: 72-170802

GREAT**OUTDOORS** PUBLISHING CO.
4747 TWENTY-EIGHTH STREET NO.
ST. PETERSBURG, FLA. 33714

Regional Key to Florida Cooking

Picture Credits

Lowis Carlton (for Fla. Dept. of Agriculture) pages 41, 56
Florida State News Bureau (Dept. of Commerce) pages 36, 37, 64, 76
McIlhenny Company page 43
United Fresh Fruit and Vegetable Assn. pages 14, 26, 50, 69

CONTENTS

FOREWORD

Like a colorful patchwork quilt, Florida's foodways are shaped from the tastes of many widely varied cultural groups—Greek and Spanish, Southern and Conch, Jewish and Minorcan, and Seminole.

What a variegated eating pattern they form! For some three hundred years after Ponce de Leon swaggered ashore north of St. Augustine to claim Florida for Spain, the state was an international pawn among nations striving to control the Gulf of Mexico.

Florida joined the Confederacy during the War Between the States, and the heavy influx of settlers from Georgia, Alabama, Louisiana and the Carolinas wove into Florida food a strong Southern strain. In most of the agricultural areas ranging from the north through the center of the state and all the way to Fort Myers and Tampa, the accent is still strongly Southern.

Out Pensacola way, Creole cooks add spice to native squash, pole beans and potatoes, and a favorite dish is gaspacho salad. Latin flavor sparks the cuisine in Tampa's Ybor City, and more recently in Miami's huge Latin colony, where Arroz con Pollo and wickedly black coffee are standouts.

Miami Beach's world-famous Jewish restaurants feature knishes, matzo ball soup and some of the world's richest desserts. And far to the south on the storied Florida Keys, Southern and Bahamian blend with Spanish in inimitable Conch cooking that works magic with seafood, coconuts and limes.

Naturally, in a peninsula with 399 miles of coastline on the Atlantic and 798 miles on the Gulf of Mexico, fish and seafood are popular. Fish is everywhere in Florida. But, again, variety is the key—from Pensacola's smoked mullet to Sarasota's pickled kingfish to Clewiston's fried catfish to Key West's conch chowder.

Meanwhile, we have an exciting assortment of traditional dishes dating back to Florida's early times as well as marvelous modern recipes. Thanks to the invaluable cooperation of food-loving Floridians up and down the state, you will find here the favorite dishes of our best cooks.

It's a rich heritage in good eating, and we invite you to sample and savor it with us.

Lowis Carlton

About the Author

Not surprisingly, since she was born in Georgia and married a native Floridian, Lowis Carlton specializes in Southern cooking. She has more than 400 cookbooks in her home, a rambling house in an avocado grove south of Miami.

More than just being interested in basic food preparation, Lowis is fascinated by people, their history, their ways of living and eating. She began in-depth study of Florida foodways during two and a half years as food editor for the Miami Herald.

Florida agriculture was the subject of country-wide newspaper columns written for the Florida Dept. of Agriculture. At that time, Lowis prepared food and arranged props. Husband Claud shot the photographs. For the past seven years, Lowis has been Food Editor for *Palm Beach Life* magazine.

A love for writing almost equal to her love for food has also led Lowis to write radio scripts, corporate publicity, advertising, and magazine articles.

She was graduated Magna Cum Laude from the University of Miami, with a Bachelor's degree and a Master's in English, and studied photography with the late Wilson Hicks, long-time *Life* magazine editor.

Her other hobbies include sewing, dancing and helping her husband feed the cows at their ranch in Arcadia.

Gates of old St. Augustine, the oldest continuously settled U. S. city, founded in 1565.

A picturesque lighthouse stands as a stately sentinel at Amelia Island along the coast of North Florida where American history really began.

In April, 1513, Ponce de Leon sailed into the harbor of yet-to-be-named St. Augustine. He was amazed and delighted at the wealth of sub-tropical flowers and foliage in this land of sunshine and blue skies. But he set sail, seeking a non-existent Fountain of Youth.

Spain sent her top-ranked admiral in 1565 to seize the harbor and all land from Labrador to Mexico. Later, the Spaniards built a string of forts from Cape Florida to Santa Elena, with St. Augustine's coquina rock structure, Castillo de San Marcos, the headquarters.

New culture arrived with a band of Minorcans late in the 1700's. These quiet, industrious people established civilized customs and higher standards of food. Dr. Andrew Turnbull brought them from the Mediterranean island, and descendants of the original groups still cook the traditional dishes.

It was not until July 10, 1821, that the Stars and Stripes fluttered over the fort, after secession of Florida from Spain. The embattled little community fought through the Seminole Indian Wars then became a "state of the American nation" in 1845.

Throughout the Seminole War from 1835 to 1842, national newspapers reported such news as how Indians were tricked into capture under a flag of truce, and the escape of Osceola's men from the dungeon in the fort. They told of the Indian leader's seizure and imprisonment while he was on his way to confer with American leaders 7 miles from St. Augustine. His death in Fort Moultrie, S.C. caused much bitterness, for public sentiment was with the Seminoles, but things calmed down when the Indian war finally ended.

The town was in Union hands from 1862 to the end of the War Between the States. There was a long slumberous period until 1874 when the first locomotive arrived and tourists began coming.

Henry M. Flagler, enchanted with the quaint air of the drowsy little Spanish town, started the renaissance of St. Augustine in 1885, with construction of the Hotel Ponce de Leon. Thus St. Augustine was launched as a winter resort. Flagler extended a railroad southward and made the city headquarters for the Florida East Coast Railway and Hotel System.

The city has never lost its atmosphere of ages past, horse-drawn carriages, the old fort, coquina rock houses with Spanish balconies, and the fanciful combination of Spanish, Minorcan and Southern food.

Seasonings were—and still are—spicy, heavy on thyme, tomatoes and onions and a fiery hot pepper called Datil, believed brought to America by the Turnbull colonists whose descendants now live in New Smyrna.

Pilau was so much in favor in time past that when it couldn't be made with chicken, pork, ham or shrimp, it was filled with speckled butter beans for a meatless main dish.

Other early-day recipes for gopher stew, clam chowder, boiled mullet and yellow rice have remained popular. At Easter, there were traditional recipes used to make treats given to street singers who serenaded the families—some sweet foods, some hot. Two favorites are Fromajardis, cheese-stuffed baked pastries, and Minorcan crispees, baked pastry circles sprinkled with cinnamon sugar.

South of St. Augustine is the lively city of Daytona Beach, famous for its 23-mile long beach of pure white, hard-packed sand. Built along the Atlantic on the Halifax River, the city began with establishment of Spanish missions late in the 16th century. Many Indians were converted to Christianity before the English conquered the area in 1702. British plantation owners were succeeded by Spanish until, finally, in the 19th century, permanent Georgia colonists built sugar plantations.

The town was named Daytona in 1870, by Mathias Day, and the word Beach was added in 1924. Pine, palmetto and cabbage palm thrive outside the city and in the spring, blossoms of orange and grapefruit groves perfume the air.

Follow the St. Johns River as it flows *north* through some of the most beautifully wooded areas of the state and you arrive at the city often called the commercial capital of Florida—Jacksonville.

It was near the mouth of the St. Johns River that Jean Ribault and a party of French Huguenot explorers anchored on April 30, 1562 marking the discovery of the river by the white man. Ribault marked the place a French possession and was followed in 1564, by 250 French Huguenot colonists.

At the foot of the hill now called St. Johns Bluff, they planted their colony and called it Fort Caroline. After Ponce de Leon claimed all Florida for Spain, Pedro Menendez was sent to wipe out the settlement, which he did. He returned in triumph to his camp, where he established the town of St. Augustine.

Because it was a good place to ford the river, the Indians called Jacksonville *Wacca Pilatka,* translated into English as Cowford. The English developed the Indian Trail from below St. Augustine to the Cowford, then to Georgia into the "King's Highway."

In 1816, Lewis Zachariah Hogans became Jacksonville's first settler, and a few frame cabins were built. Late in June, 1822, the town was surveyed, named in honor of General Andrew Jackson. At the end of the Seminole War in 1842, the city began its climb to its modern status as a leader among Florida cities.

Today, it is a lively center for industry, insurance and transportation.

But like so many north Florida cities, it has retained an old-time Southern charm with its large, palatial homes, lushly landscaped parks and—most of all—enormous, moss-draped oaks and pines.

Home port for a big shrimp fleet is Mayport on Jacksonville Beach. Seafood of all kinds is extremely popular, but don't expect to find frozen mullet stew at the market!

MINORCAN AND OLD ST. AUGUSTINE RECIPES

FROMAJARDIS CHEESE CAKES

These Minorcan cakes play an important part in a popular St. Augustine tradition. On Easter Eve, the Fromajardis folk song was sung by strolling men singers in serenade to a house. If these cheese cakes and wine were served in abundance by the household, the singers sang their praises, then went to sit on the seawall and enjoy the refreshments. If no cakes were forthcoming, the singers did not hesitate to sing out their criticism of the stingy man, to the delight of the neighbors.

For days before Easter, women were busy baking, preparing not less than half a flour barrel of the cheese cakes. In the spring of 1843, William Cullen Bryant heard the singers during a St. Augustine visit. He wrote the Mahonese dialect version of their song in his "Letters of a Traveller."

FROMAJARDIS

rich pie dough	4 well beaten eggs
pinch of nutmeg	⅛ teaspoon salt
½ pound aged Cheddar cheese	¼ teaspoon cayenne pepper

Prepare pie dough, blending in nutmeg. Roll dough thin. Cut in rounds the size of a saucer. On one half of round, cut a cross. Grate cheese. Beat in eggs, salt, pepper. Place 1 spoonful of this on unslashed half of dough circle. Fold to make half-circle; pinch edges together. Brush with melted butter. Bake in 375 deg. oven until golden brown. Cheese will puff up through the cross. Serve with Florida orange wine.

PEACH JAM CAKE

1 cup white raisins, soaked in
    peach brandy
1 cup butter or margarine
2 cups sugar
3 eggs, separated
1 cup peach jam
3½ cups flour

½ teaspoon salt
1½ teaspoons baking powder
1 teaspoon each cinnamon, nutmeg,
    allspice and ginger
1 teaspoon soda
1 cup buttermilk
1 cup chopped pecans

Place raisins in brandy and let stand overnight. Cream butter and sugar until light. Add egg yolks; mix well. Add jam and beat until smooth. Sift together twice the flour, salt, baking powder and spices. Stir soda into buttermilk. Add milk to creamed mixture alternately with flour, stirring to blend well each time. Toss nuts and raisins in a little flour; fold into cake mixture. Beat egg whites until stiff and fold in. Pour into oiled tube pan and bake at 350 deg. about 45 minutes, or until done.

CHICKEN PILAU (pronounced Pur-lo)

½ pound diced white bacon
3½ pound hen
½ cup water
¼ cup chopped green pepper
4 medium onions, chopped fine
1 clove finely chopped garlic
4 cups canned tomatoes

¼ teaspoon thyme
2 teaspoons salt
⅛ teaspoon pepper
6 cups long grain rice
6 cups water
1 hot green (Datil) pepper, chopped

Cut chicken and brown in deep fat in large, heavy iron pot. Drain off grease and add ½ cup water. Cover; place over low heat to simmer. Fry bacon; then in grease with garlic fry chopped onions and peppers until tender but not brown. Add tomatoes, thyme, salt, pepper, bacon to chicken. Cover and simmer about 2 hours, or until chicken is tender. During cooking, add more water if needed. Now measure liquid in pot and add enough water to make 6 cups liquid. Pour back into pot, add rice to chicken mixture. Cover; cook over low heat until rice is done. Fifteen minutes before it is done, add chopped hot pepper. Makes 8 servings.

MINORCAN CHRISTMAS CANDY

3 cups freshly grated coconut
2 cups granulated sugar

½ cup coconut milk
3 tablespoons white Karo syrup

Stir coconut, sugar and milk to blend well; add syrup. Over very low heat, cook, stirring constantly until mixture becomes thick and heavy. Drop in small teaspoonfuls onto waxed paper and allow to harden. (Note: If prepared coconut is used, soak ¼ cup coconut in warm milk for 1 hour, then strain, to get coconut milk.)

NORTHEAST FLORIDA SPECIALTIES

LEMON BAKED CHICKEN WITH SPICED PEACHES

1 broiler-fryer chicken, quartered
1 tablespoon flour
1 teaspoon Ac'cent
½ teaspoon salt

⅛ teaspoon pepper
½ teaspoon paprika
1 tablespoon butter or margarine
3 tablespoons lemon or lime juice

Place chicken in shallow baking dish. Combine flour, Ac'cent, salt, pepper, paprika; sprinkle over chicken. Dot with butter. Bake uncovered at 375 deg. 30 minutes. Sprinkle with lemon juice; bake 20 minutes longer. (Note to dieters: only 200 calories per serving.) Serve with spiced peaches:

1 29-oz. can cling peach hlaves   1/3 cup brown sugar
1 teaspoon whole cloves   ¼ cup lemon or lime juice

Drain peach syrup into saucepan. Stud peach halves with half the cloves; reserve. Bring syrup and remaining cloves to a boil; boil rapidly until reduced to ½ cup. Add sugar, lemon juice and peaches; bring to a boil. Remove from heat. Serve warm with chicken. Makes 6 servings.

SOUTHERN BARBECUED CHICKEN

3 dressed young broilers, split   ¼ teaspoon Tabasco sauce
2 tablespoons catsup   2 tablespoons Worcestershire
2 tablespoons vinegar   2 tablespoons water
½ teaspoon dry mustard   5 tablespoons melted butter
1 tablespoon lemon or lime juice   ½ teaspoon paprika

Rub each broiler half with salt, pepper, melted butter. Place on broiler rack, skin face down and cook under moderate heat until brown and almost tender. Turn and cook other side. Mix ingredients and use to baste chicken frequently during broiling. Makes 6 servings.

BARBECUED SHRIMP

2 pounds raw shrimp   ½ cup hot water
1/3 cup minced onion   2 teaspoons prepared mustard
3 tablespoons olive oil   2 tablespoons Worcestershire sauce
1 cup catsup   ¼ teaspoon salt
1/3 cup lemon juice   1 teaspoon chili sauce
2 tablespoons brown sugar

In heavy pan, saute onion in olive oil until transparent. Peel and de-vein shrimp. Add all remaining ingredients except shrimp to onion in pan. Turn heat low; cover and simmer 10 minutes. Place shrimp on broiling platter; cover with sauce. With shrimp 6 inches below broiler, broil about 6 minutes or until shrimp are cooked. Turn once. Serve hot with remaining sauce. Serves 4.

ROAST PORK, SPANISH STYLE

6 pound pork loin roast   ¼ teaspoon pepper
2 garlic buds   4 tablespoons oregano
1 teaspoon salt   2/3 cup fresh lime juice

Cut garlic into slivers; make slits all over the roast and insert garlic. Combine salt, pepper and oregano. Rub this over the meat. Place fat side up on a rack pan in preheated 450 deg. oven; immediately reduce heat to 350 deg. and cook uncovered 30 to 35 minutes to the pound. If a meat thermometer is used, it should read 185 deg. When pork begins to brown baste frequently with lime juice. (This roast has slight garlic flavor with a crisp, tart crust.) Serve with spiced crabapples.

FLORIDA VEGETABLES

BROCCOLI SOUFFLE WITH CHEESE SAUCE

4 tablespoons butter or margarine,
   divided
3 tablespoons cornstarch
1 cup beef bouillon
2 teaspoons lemon juice
½ teaspoon salt
¼ teaspoon Tabasco sauce
⅛ teaspoon nutmeg

4 egg yolks
1/3 cup grated Parmesan cheese
2 tablespoons chopped scallions
1 10-oz. package frozen chopped broccoli, thawed—or fresh broccoli,
   cooked
5 egg whites
½ teaspoon cream of tartar

Melt 3 tablespoons butter in pan; blend in cornstarch. Gradually stir in bouillon. Cook, stirring constantly, until mixture thickens and comes to a boil. Remove from heat. Stir in lemon juice, salt, Tabasco and nutmeg. Beat egg yolks in small bowl and stir in a little hot sauce. Stir into remaining sauce and add grated cheese. Melt remaining 1 tablespoon butter in skillet; add scallions and cook until tender. Add thawed broccoli; stir over moderately high heat until moisture evaporates, then add to sauce.

Beat egg whites with cream of tartar until stiff but not dry. Stir ¼ of beaten whites into broccoli sauce; mix well. Fold in remaining whites, mixing as little as possible. Turn into buttered 1½-quart souffle dish and sprinkle top with more grated Parmesan cheese. Bake in 375 deg. oven 35 to 40 minutes until top is puffed and browned. (Center will be moist; for a drier, firmer center bake until a knife inserted in center comes out clean.) Serve with cheese sauce. Serves 6.

Cheese Sauce: 2 tablespoons butter; 2 tablespoons flour; ½ teaspoon salt; ¼ teaspoon Tabasco; ⅛ teaspoon dry mustard; 1½ cups milk; 1 cup shredded Cheddar cheese.

Melt butter in pan; blend in flour and seasonings. Stir in milk. Cook, stirring constantly, until thickens and comes to a boil. Cook 2 minutes longer, stirring constantly. Add cheese; stir until melted.

CUCUMBER SAUCE FOR FISH OR SALAD

1 cup sour cream
½ cup seeded, grated cucumber
½ teaspoon salt

1 teaspoon finely chopped fresh dill
2 teaspoons finely chopped chives
½ teaspoon black pepper

Combine cream with cucumber, salt, dill, chives and pepper. Blend well and refrigerate 1 to 2 hours before serving.

CORN PUDDING, SOUTHERN STYLE

(A real, old fashioned Southern dinner would include fried chicken with gravy, rice, corn pudding, sliced ripe tomato salad, hot biscuit with guava jelly. For dessert, a richly frosted Lane Cake or homemade peach ice cream.) (Corn pudding and barbecued chicken were traditional partners at political gatherings in the early South.)

2 cups milk
2 cups corn cut from the cob
1/4 cup melted butter
1 tablespoon sugar

1 teaspoon salt
1/4 teaspoon pepper
3 well beaten eggs

Combine milk and corn in saucepan and heat. Beat eggs; set aside. Add to milk and corn the butter, sugar and seasonings. Pour a little corn mixture over the beaten eggs. Beat this, then return to corn mixture. Stir and cook for several minutes. Turn into a greased casserole and bake in 350 deg. oven about 45 minutes, or until pudding sets. Serves 6.

RED AND WHITE TOMATO MOLDED SALAD

1 envelope gelatin
1/2 cup cold tomato juice
1 1/4 cups hot tomato juice

1/2 teaspoon salt
1 tablespoon lemon juice
egg salad layer

Soften gelatin in 2 tablespoons cold tomato juice. Stir in remaining cold, then hot tomato juice. When dissolved, mix in salt and lemon juice. Pour into oiled loaf pan; refrigerate until almost firm; add egg layer. Chill until set; unmold and serve with mayonnaise mixed with mashed avocado.

EGG SALAD LAYER

1 envelope gelatin
1/2 cup cold water
1 teaspoon salt
2 tablespoons lemon juice
1/2 teaspoon Worcestershire
3/4 cup mayonnaise

2 teaspoons grated onion
1/2 cup finely chopped celery
1/4 cup finely chopped green pepper
1 tablespoon celery seed
1/4 cup finely chopped pimiento
4 chopped hard-cooked eggs

Soften gelatin in cold water. Place in top of double boiler and heat until dissolved, stirring slowly. Add salt, lemon juice, Worcestershire and pepper. Cool. Add mayonnaise and remaining ingredients, stirring until well blended. Place atop firm tomato layer in loaf pan. Serves 8.

HOT BOLLOS, SPANISH STYLE

2 pounds dried black eyed peas
3 cloves garlic
3 tablespoons scraped onion
1 teaspoon salt

1/4 teaspoon pepper
seeds of small, dried hot pepper
water
olive or cooking oil

Wash and pick peas; soak overnight in cold water. Rub peas against sides of a sieve until hulls come off. Wash again, scooping off hulls that float on top. Drain peas, mix with other ingredients except cooking oil. Run through food chopper fine blade. Add enough water to make a thick paste; form into small balls. Fry in deep fat, about 375 deg., until golden brown. Serve as a hot appetizer. (Recipe borrowed from Cubans in Key West, where hot Bollos are still sold on street corners.)

Lemon gives a tropical taste to Frosty Lemon Milk Sherbet.

DESSERTS

FROSTY LEMON MILK SHERBET

2 cups evaporated milk
1½ cups sugar
2 cups water
2 tablespoons chopped fresh mint
½ cup fresh lemon juice

¾ teaspoon grated fresh lemon rind
2 teaspoons vanilla
½ teaspoon ground mace
⅛ teaspoon salt
grated fresh lemon rind

Pour evaporated milk into freezing tray. Place in freezer and chill until frozen around sides, about 1 hour. Combine sugar, water and fresh mint in pan. Bring to boiling point; boil 2-3 minutes. Remove from heat; cool. Stir in lemon juice, lemon rind, vanilla, ground mace and salt. Turn into freezing tray and freeze to a mush, about 1 hour. Whip partially frozen evaporated milk until thick and fluffy. Gradually beat in frozen lemon mixture. Return to 2 freezing trays and freeze until firm. Garnish with grated lemon rind. Makes 8 servings.

BANANA-RUM PUDDING WITH MERINGUE

3 cups milk
1/3 cup cornstarch
1 cup sugar
¾ teaspoon salt
3 eggs, separated

1 teaspoon vanilla
1 teaspoon rum flavoring
26 small vanilla wafers
3 large ripe bananas

Scald milk in top of double boiler; pour slowly over cornstarch mixed with 2/3 cup sugar and ½ teaspoon salt. Cook over boiling water, stirring constantly until mixture thickens. Cover; cook 15 minutes, stirring occasionally. Add hot mixture very slowly to beaten egg yolks, stirring constantly. Return to double boiler; cook 2 minutes. Cool; add vanilla and rum flavorings. In 1½ quart casserole, place alternate layers of wafers, bananas and pudding, ending with pudding. Add ¼ teaspoon salt to egg whites; beat until foamy. Beat in 1/3 cup sugar gradually, beating until soft peaks form. Pile on pudding; bake in 350 deg. oven 15 minutes till light brown. Chill before serving. Makes 6 servings.

PAPAYA NUT PIE

1 cup orange juice	1½ cups diced papaya, fresh or canned
2 tablespoons cornstarch	1 baked 9-inch pie shell
¼ cup sugar	whipped cream
Juice of 1 lemon	toasted coconut
½ teaspoon ground ginger	

Blend orange juice, cornstarch, sugar and lemon and ginger; heat slowly in pan, stirring constantly until thick and clear. Cool slightly. Pour over papaya cubes placed in baked pie shell. Refrigerate and chill well. Swirl whipped cream on top and sprinkle with toasted coconut at serving time.

GUAVA SHELLS WITH CREAM CHEESE

One of the most delicious—and wonderfully simple—desserts in Florida is a gift from Spanish settlers. Pretty pink canned guava shells are sold in the gourmet section of most grocery stores. Simply open them, serve with or without the spicy juice with a generous wedge of cream cheese. If you like, add a very salty crisp cracker for flavor contrast. A compliment-winner!

Excitement was high when the first automobile traveled from Jacksonville to Miami in five days, in 1908.

Indians lived near Biscayne Bay in 1513, we know, because Ponce de Leon reported seeing them when he sailed into the Bay and discovered Cape Florida. Some bones and broken tools found date back to 400-1400 A.D. At the mouth of the clear blue Miami River, a group of missionaries settled in 1568, and soldiers built Fort Dallas there in 1836.

But the Keys area was where the action was. A handful of people attempted to start a coconut plantation among the mangroves, seagrape and scrub palmetto of Miami Beach in 1882. But insects plagued the workers; rats and rabbits ate the young tree shoots; and by 1890 it was given up as a failure. Happily, enough trees survived to make Miami Beach a palm-fringed island.

In Miami, meanwhile, William Brickell built a home on the river's south shore while Julia Tuttle settled on the north side. She was the lady who put Miami on the map the day she cut an orange blossom, packed it in damp cotton and sent it to Henry Flagler in north Florida. This ambitious lady had been urging him to extend his railroad to Miami but he ignored her until the winter of 1894 when a hard freeze killed north Florida citrus.

The blossoms lured Flagler southward where he verified that Miami was indeed basking in the sunshine far from icy breezes. He accepted gifts of land from Mrs. Tuttle and other residents, and his railroad was built. It was to bring guests to his new wooden Royal Palm Hotel in Miami as it did to his Ponce de Leon in St. Augustine and his Royal Poinciana in Palm Beach.

While millionaires were enjoying bay breezes at Flagler's Royal Palm Hotel, the Beach was beginning to stir into life. Some dredging was done and the longest wooden bridge in the nation was begun by John S. Collins, then stopped when funds ran out. Millionaire promoter Carl F. Fisher of Indianapolis loaned him $50,000 with 200 acres of land as security, and the bridge was completed.

Fisher's promotional genius lured wealthy men south, persuaded them to invest, and began the development of land and building of hotels.

In the early 1920's, people by the millions came to Miami and Miami Beach, eager to make a fortune in the fantastic Florida land boom which peaked in 1925. To the Southerners who had made their home were added Latins and people from industrial centers in the north and midwest.

When the railroad broke down and a ship sank blocking the harbor, preventing delivery of tons of building supplies, the boom went bust in 1926. The final misfortune was the great hurricane of Sept. 18, 1926. It wiped out homes, killed hundreds, and pushed water from the ocean over to the Bay.

Tourism—based on the new idea of package vacations for moderate-income families—revived the area and brought back a prosperity that has seldom faltered. Air conditioning extended the vacation season from winter throughout the summer. And the population continued to climb.

One of the nation's largest Jewish communities began growing on the Beach; by 1947, nearly half the permanent population was Jewish. Refugees fleeing Castro's regime flowed into Miami by the hundreds of thousands. The imprint of both groups is reflected in the communities, and especially in the many fine Jewish and Spanish restaurants in south Florida.

Follow the beach from Miami Beach and you reach Fort Lauderdale, the boating capital of the world, with 135 miles of waterways. Here is Port Everglades, deepest harbor on the east Florida coast. The city was named to honor Major William Lauderdale, who commanded the local fort during the Seminole War.

The wide white beach leads north to Palm Beach. Great mansions drowse in the beautiful seaside resort where Flagler built his hotel for millionaires in 1893. Addison Mizner's architectural touch remains, revealed in the mellow-toned red tile roofs and Spanish arches of the aging but still beautiful mansions. Worth Avenue is still one of the world's most beautiful streets.

Though it remains a favorite spot with many of America's socialites, inflation has struck and many of the great homes of Palm Beach have become museums or have been replaced by commercial buildings. But the food in elegant Palm Beach restaurants is still among the world's best.

Northward the beach curves inward beside Fort Pierce, Melbourne and to John F. Kennedy Space Center where space shots made recent history. Directly west lies the Orlando area with Florida's great tourist attraction, fabulous Disney World.

South Florida's food is a world unto itself. The nation's only true sub-tropical area produces exotic mangoes, avocadoes, limes, litchee nuts, coconuts, as well as a full array of winter vegetables. Seafood is plentiful, with stone crabs, lobster, red snapper, and mackerel among the favorites.

The influx of tourists seeking gourmet food has sparked the growth of fine restaurants, and at Miami Beach, there are French and Italian, Jewish and Spanish, and dozens more. The nation's greatest chefs practice their art in the luxury hotels on both sides of Biscayne Bay. In a word, Miami has become cosmopolitan in its taste.

SPANISH SPECIALTIES
FRIJOLES NEGROS A LA CUBANA (Cuban Black Beans)

2 cups (1 lb.) black beans	1 bay leaf
water to cover 1 inch above beans	1 minced green pepper
½ teaspoon salt, or to taste	1 chopped onion
1 clove garlic, cut in half	1 tablespoon cider vinegar
2 tablespoons cooking oil (olive oil)	salt, pepper to taste
3 cloves garlic, mashed	

Wash and pick beans. Place in covered pot with enough water to stand 1 inch above beans. Soak overnight. Add salt and cook beans until tender, adding garlic. Meanwhile, to make sauce, heat oil in heavy frypan and add mashed garlic, bay leaf, green pepper and onion. Simmer 5 minutes, add vinegar and salt to taste. Continue cooking sauce until thickened. Mix with beans, re-heat, and serve with fluffy white rice. Serves 6.

EGGS IN SPANISH SAUCE

1 29-oz. can tomatoes	½ bay leaf
1 sliced onion	2 tablespoons butter or margarine
1 teaspoon sugar	2 tablespoons flour
¾ teaspoon Tabasco	3 cups cooked rice
¾ teaspoon salt	6 eggs
⅛ teaspoon ground cloves	¼ cup grated cheddar cheese

Simmer tomatoes, onion, sugar, Tabasco, salt, cloves and bay leaf in saucepan about 10 minutes. Remove bay leaf. Blend butter and flour together. Add to tomato mixture. Cook, stirring constantly, until thickened. Spread rice in greased shallow 2½-quart casserole, making 6 hollows in it with a tablespoon. Break an egg into each nest. Carefully pour sauce over all. Sprinkle with cheese. Bake in 350 deg. F. oven 20 minutes or until the eggs are firm. Makes 6 servings. (Note: Combining rice with eggs in this fashion is popular in old Spain as well as the Spanish-speaking lands south of Florida.)

CUBAN FLAN (Caramel Custard)

½ cup sugar	2 cups milk
1 teaspoon water	4 egg yolks
pinch of salt	½ teaspoon vanilla

In skillet, over very low heat, place 6 tablespoons sugar and the water and cook until sugar turns to golden syrup. Stir occasionally to prevent burning. Pour into 4 custard cups and cool until firm. Beat together milk, beaten egg yolks, vanilla and 2 tablespoons sugar until thoroughly blended. Pour over caramel in custard cups. Pour ½ inch boiling water in deep pan; place cups in water. Bake at 325 deg. about 1 hour 15 minutes, or until knife slipped into center comes out clean. Chill well. Invert onto chilled plates to serve. Makes 4 servings.

GREEN BANANA PUREE

6 large green firm cooking bananas	4 cups water
lemon juice	½ teaspoon salt

Peel green bananas; scrape then rub them with lemon juice. Boil in salted water until tender. Drain and mash. Serve in a mound on a hot dish to accompany meats. Makes 6 servings.

GOLD-COAST GOURMET

CHICKEN AVOCADO CREPES

½ cup ripe olives, chopped	salt, pepper
5 tablespoons butter	2 cups diced cooked chicken
5 tablespoons flour	2 eggs
1 cup cream (or undiluted	2/3 cup milk
evaporated milk)	½ cup sifted flour
1 cup chicken broth	½ teaspoon salt
¾ cup dry white wine	1 tablespoon melted butter
1 cup grated process Swiss cheese	avocado, large size, peeled and sliced
½ teaspoon Worcestershire sauce	paprika; ripe olives
2 tablespoons chopped parsley	

In large saucepan, melt 5 tablespoons butter and blend in 5 tablespoons flour. Pour in cream, broth and wine. Cook, stirring constantly, until it boils and thickens. Stir in until smooth ¾ cup cheese, Worcestershire sauce, parsley and salt and pepper to taste. Measure 1 cup sauce and add olives and chicken.

To make pancakes, beat eggs lightly, combine with milk. Sift ½ cup flour with ½ teaspoon salt. Combine with egg mixture; beat till smooth. Blend in butter. In lightly greased frypan, pour 4 tablespoons batter; tilt pan to spread. Bake until golden brown, turning once. Repeat.

In greased baking dish, place pancakes which have been filled with sauce, rolled and secured with toothpick. Pour remaining sauce over pancakes; sprinkle with remaining cheese and paprika. Bake in 375 deg. oven 15 minutes; add a couple of minutes under the broiler to brown. Top pancakes with sliced avocado and whole ripe olives. Makes 6 servings.

CURRIED EGG MOLD

2 envelopes unflavored gelatin
½ cup cold water
2 cups rich chicken stock, boiling
1 tablespoon curry powder

1½ cups mayonnaise
3 sliced hard-cooked eggs
6 sliced stuffed olives
½ cup finely sliced celery

Sprinkle gelatin on cold water till soft. Add gelatin mixture to chicken stock with curry powder. Stir to dissolve. Chill till slightly thick. Gradually stir in mayonnaise until blended. Mix in eggs, olives, celery. Season to taste with salt and pepper. Turn into oiled 1½-qt. ring mold. Chill till firm; unmold on greens. If desired, garnish with green mayonnaise and black olives. Makes 6-8 servings.

JFK SALAD DRESSING

(Created by Fontainebleau Hotel chef at Miami Beach for John F. Kennedy.)

5 whole eggs
1 clove garlic
1 teaspoon salt
¼ teaspoon pepper
2 tablespoons paprika

1 teaspoon prepared mustard
3 cups salad oil
1 cup olive oil
½ cup red wine vinegar

Crack eggs into bowl. Crush garlic and add. Combine with salt, pepper, paprika and mustard; mix well. Add oils slowly, beating constantly. If mixture gets too thick, add a little vinegar. Continue beating, add all of the vinegar until thoroughly blended. Correct salt, pepper to taste.

ITALIAN MEAT LOAF

3 slices white bread
3 slices rye bread
1¼ cups beef stock
4 tablespoons minced onion
1 tablespoon prepared mustard
2 teaspoons salt

½ teaspoon parsley flakes
⅛ teaspoon black pepper
¼ cup parmesan cheese
2 eggs
2 pounds ground beef
1 tablespoon butter

Break bread into pieces in large mixing bowl. Add beef stock and onion. Let stand 10 minutes. With fork, mash bread pieces and beat mixture well. Add mustard, salt, parsley flakes, pepper, cheese, eggs. Beat well with a fork. Add beef; mix thoroughly. Pack into oiled 9x5-inch loaf pan. Dot top with butter. Bake in 375 deg. oven 60-70 minutes. Makes 8 servings.

HAM-CHEESE FONDUE SOUFFLE

3 cups cubed French or Italian bread
3 cups cubed cooked ham
½ pound Cheddar cheese in 1-inch cubes
3 tablespoons flour
1 tablespoon dry mustard
3 tablespoons melted butter
4 eggs
3 cups milk
few drops red hot sauce

Butter an 8-cup straight side casserole dish. In bottom place layer of cubed bread, then layer of ham, layer of cubed cheese. Mix flour with mustard; sprinkle over cheese. Drizzle butter or margarine over top. Beat eggs, add milk and red hot sauce; pour over layers. Cover; chill at least 4 hours, preferably overnight. Bake uncovered in 350 deg. oven 1 hour. Serve at once. (Secret of this dish is the long chilling.) Makes 6 servings.

JEWISH SPECIALTIES

SAUERBRATEN WITH POTATO PANCAKES

4 pounds round steak
1 pint cider vinegar
water
3 bay leaves
3 peppercorns
2 tablespoons flour
salt, pepper, paprika
1 teaspoon allspice
2 tablespoons fat
6 carrots
6 onions, sliced
12 gingersnaps
1 tablespoon sugar

Place meat in bowl, pour over vinegar and enough water to cover. Add bay leaves and peppercorns. Refrigerate 3 days. Combine flour, salt, pepper, paprika and allspice. Drain meat; shake in bag filled with flour mixture. Brown meat lightly in hot fat. Place meat in heavy saucepan with sliced carrots, onions and 2 cups of vinegar marinade. Cover and simmer 2 hours. Crumble gingersnaps, add with sugar to liquid around meat. Add salt and pepper to taste. Serve with potato pancakes. Makes 6-8 servings.

POTATO PANCAKES (Latkes)

2 cups raw grated potatoes
2 well beaten eggs
1 tablespoon flour or matzo meal
pinch baking powder
1 tablespoon grated onion
salt, pepper to taste

Peel and grate potatoes. Thoroughly combine all ingredients. Drop by tablespoonful into hot oil in frying pan. Fry until crisp at edges on under side; turn and fry until done. Makes 4 servings.

PASSOVER JELLY ROLL

½ cup sifted matzo cake meal
½ cup potato flour
6 eggs, separated
1 cup sugar
juice and rind of ½ lemon
2 tablespoons cold water
¼ teaspoon salt
1 cup raspberry preserves
confectioners sugar

Line shallow 10x15-inch jelly roll pan with wax paper. Sift together matzo cake meal and potato flour. Beat egg yolks with sugar until thick and lemon colored. Stir in lemon juice, grated rind and water. Gradually add sifted dry ingredients, stirring to make thick batter. Beat egg whites and salt until stiff but not dry. Fold gently into batter.

Turn into jelly roll pan. Bake in 325 deg. oven about 20 minutes or until just done. Don't let edges brown and harden. Remove from oven; peel off paper. Turn onto a towel which has been spread with sugar. Trim off crisp edges. Roll cake in towel; cool completely. Unroll. Remove towel. Spread with preserves. Roll again; dust lightly with confectioners sugar. Serves 10.

QUICK BLINI (Russian Pancakes)

¾ cup sifted all purpose flour	½ cup milk
1/3 teaspoon baking powder	1 slightly beaten egg
¼ teaspoon salt	2 tablespoons sour cream

Sift together twice flour, baking powder, salt. Stir in all ingredients; mix well. Drop by tablespoon to make very small pancakes, 2 inches or less wide, and very thin. Brown on hot griddle; turn once. Serve with sour cream. Makes 25-30 pancakes.

TROPICAL FRUIT SPECIALTIES

CARACAS PINEAPPLE COUPE

2 fresh pineapples	1 pint orange sherbet
1 cantaloupe	1 pint lime sherbet
¼ cup maraschino cordial	¼ cup shredded coconut
¼ cup Cointreau cordial	½ pint whipped cream

Cut pineapples in half lengthwise; scoop out, leaving ½-inch border of fruit around edge. Dice scooped out pineapple. Cut cantaloupe, clean, and cut melon meat into balls or cubes. Combine the two cordials, pineapple and cantaloupe and refrigerate for 4 hours. Fill pineapple shells with fruit. Top with orange and lime sherbets, sprinkle with shredded coconut and circle with whipped cream. Makes 4 large servings.

MANGO (OR PEACH) FROST

Deceptively simple, this recipe is an all-time favorite. Specially good after a heavy meal, it has marvelous tropical flavor and a texture like soft sherbet.

1 heaping cup sliced mangoes (or peaches)	1 tablespoon sugar
2 tablespoons powdered milk	1 tablespoon light rum
juice of 1 lime	crushed ice

Combine first 5 ingredients in blender. Add crushed ice to fill container. Blend at high speed until mixture thickens to the consistency of soft sherbet. Serve immediately topped with a sprig of mint, with a spoon or straw, depending on thickness.

GUAVA CHEESE PIE

½ cup guava paste	1 tablespoon lime juice
½ cup cream	pinch of salt
3 eggs	1 8-inch graham cracker crumb crust
1 pound sieved cottage cheese	dash of mace

Chop guava paste into small cubes. Heat in cream over lowest possible heat until paste partially melts but tiny blobs of paste remain. Beat eggs well until fluffy and lemon colored. Add to cheese together with guava mixture, lime juice, salt. Pour into crumb crust; sprinkle with mace. Bake in 350 deg. F. oven 45 to 55 minutes. Makes 1 8-inch pie.

LIME FRENCH DRESSING FOR VEGETABLES

5 tablespoons salad oil
½ teaspoon salt
½ teaspoon paprika
½ teaspoon prepared mustard

6 tablespoons lime juice
1 teaspoon onion juice
¼ teaspoon garlic salt

Place all ingredients in small bottle; cover tightly and shake well. Chill. Place in blender just before serving. Makes ¾ cup of tart dressing perfect with greens, avocadoes or vegetable combinations.

LIME DESSERT SAUCE

1 tablespoon cornstarch
½ cup sugar
cold water

¾ cup boiling water
2 tablespoons butter or margarine
2½ tablespoons lime juice

Mix cornstarch with sugar. Blend to smooth paste with a little cold water. Gradually stir paste into boiling water. Continue stirring over moderate heat until thickened. Remove from fire. Add butter and lime juice. Tangy sweet sauce delicious hot or cold, over pudding or fritters.

FLORIDA GREEN ICE CREAM

1 medium avocado, de-seeded,
   mashed (¾ cup of pulp)
2/3 cup sugar
3½ tablespoons lime juice

1 cup pineapple juice
½ teaspoon salt
1½ cups light cream

Stir all ingredients together till thoroughly blended. Freeze in ice cube tray till almost firm. Break up and whip till light and fluffy. Turn into fancy 1-quart mold and re-freeze 2 hours or till firm. Makes 6 servings.

CREAM OF AVOCADO SOUP

1 quart thin white sauce
1 cup finely mashed avocado
1/6 teaspoon ginger
pinch of salt

grated rind of 1 orange
2 tablespoons whipped cream
paprika
thin slices of avocado

Combine white sauce, avocado, ginger, salt and orange rind. Beat until well blended. Heat. Just before serving, add whipped cream, dash of paprika and thin slices of avocado. Serves 6.

PRIZE-WINNING SHRIMP STUFFED AVOCADOES

3 large avocadoes
3 tablespoons lime juice
1 teaspoon salt
4 tablespoons butter
6 tablespoons flour
⅛ teaspoon black pepper

1½ cups milk
½ cup cooked sliced celery
¼ cup minced pimiento
1 cup boiled shrimp
2/3 cup grated Cheddar cheese

Cut avocadoes lengthwise into halves; peel. Sprinkle with lime juice and
½ teaspoon salt. Melt butter, blend in flour, add remaining salt, pepper and milk;
cook until thickened, stirring constantly. Add celery, pimiento and shrimp. Fill
avocadoes with shrimp mixture; cover with grated cheese, place in baking pan.
Pour in boiling water to depth of ½ inch and bake in 350 deg. F. oven 15 minutes.
Serves 6.

KUMQUAT (OR CALAMONDIN) MARMALADE

1 quart halved, seeded kumquats   1 cup sugar to each cup fruit
water to cover fruit   juice of ½ lemon

Place halved, seeded fruit in water to cover; cook until skin is soft. Leave
fruit in pan, cover and let soak in juices overnight. Measure 1 cup sugar to each
cup of fruit. Add juice of ½ lemon (or whole lemon for added tartness). Cook
at very high speed until it boils then start stirring and cook, stirring constantly,
15 minutes—but never more than 20 minutes! This makes a marmalade of soft
consistency. Pour into jars and seal.

SURINAM CHERRY JAM

3¾ cups sugar   3¾ cups seeded Florida Surinam
2 cups water   cherries

Combine sugar and water, bring to boil and add cherries. Boil cherries in
syrup 20-25 minutes, or until juice thickens slightly but does not jell. Pour into
hot jars and seal.

FREEZING MANGOES

Use high quality mangoes at peak of ripeness. Peel and cut from seed in
slices. Pack into moisture-vapor-proof containers, packing down to eliminate air
spaces. Leave ¾ inch space at top. Pour sweetened limeade over to cover. (This
prevents fruit from drying out and losing texture and flavor.) Seal and freeze
against walls of home freezer.

MANGO CHUTNEY, INDIAN STYLE

4 pounds green mangoes   4 teaspoons allspice
2 quarts vinegar   2 cups dark raisins
2 pounds sugar   1 clove garlic
2 tablespoons white mustard seed   1 pound preserved ginger in syrup
1 tablespoon ground dried chili pepper

Peel and cut fruit; add 1 quart vinegar. Boil 20 minutes. Combine sugar
and second quart of vinegar and boil until thick syrup forms, about 1 hour. Pour
off most of the liquid from fruit and add to this syrup. Boil this combination
until thickened, about 15 minutes. Combine this thick syrup with rest of the
ingredients and fruit except ginger; cook 30 minutes. Add chopped ginger and its
syrup; cook 10 minutes longer. Remove garlic. Pour into sterilized jars and seal.
To improve flavor, let stand in the sun for three days. Makes about 4 quarts.

BANANAS FLAMBE

3 tablespoons butter   ¼ cup banana liqueur
2 tablespoons brown sugar   ¼ cup light rum
3 bananas, peeled, sliced lengthwise   2 tablespoons brandy

Melt butter in chafing dish or frypan. Add brown sugar and cook until bubbling and syrupy. Put in sliced bananas, roll in sauce and spoon sauce over until glazed. Push bananas to one side; heat other side of pan until it is dry. Pour in banana liqueur; ignite. Spoon flaming liqueur over fruit until flames die. Repeat with rum, then brandy, each time letting flames die. Serve over vanilla ice cream. Makes 3 servings.

VAL MAYFIELD'S TROPICAL FRUIT PIE

Crust:
2 cups fine almond macaroon crumbs
¼ cup confectioners sugar
½ cup melted butter or margarine
Filling:
1 cup crushed pineapple
2 tablespoons flour
3 tablespoons sugar

1 cup fresh or frozen coconut
2 tablespoons sugar
½ teaspoon coconut flavoring
2 large bananas brushed with lemon
    juice
1 cup whipped cream
maraschino cherries

In medium bowl, with fork toss macaroon crumbs, sugar and butter until well mixed. Press into bottom and sides of 8-inch pie plate. Refrigerate. Combine pineapple, flour and sugar in saucepan and cook over medium heat until thickened, stirring constantly, about 10 minutes. Cool.

To open fresh coconut, make a hole in the eye and drain milk. Place nut in 350 deg. oven 20 minutes. Remove; let cool. Wrap in towel and crack with hammer. One easy pull and the meat is off. Peel brown skin; grate coconut. Mix with sugar and flavoring. Set aside ½ cup; toast this lightly in 250 deg. oven.

In bottom of pie crust, place sliced bananas. Over this, spread cooled pineapple mixture. Cover with one cup untoasted coconut. Top with whipped cream. Sprinkle with ½ cup toasted coconut. Refrigerate. Before serving, garnish with maraschino cherries. Makes one 8-inch pie.

PINEAPPLE CHEESE DIP

1 8-oz. carton whipped cream cheese
2 cups shredded Cheddar cheese
¼ cup milk
3 tablespoons port wine (or grape
    juice)

1 teaspoon Worcestershire sauce
½ teaspoon salt
½ teaspoon dry mustard
1 ripe sweet pineapple

Beat together cheeses, milk, wine, Worcestershire sauce, salt, and dry mustard in bowl. Cut pineapple in half crosswise and cut pineapple meat out of bottom half to make a shell; cut into cubes. Fill shell with cheese mixture. Refrigerate until ready to serve. Cut crown off top half of pineapple, cut off rind, cut into quarters, cut away core and cut meat into chunks. Refrigerate. Let cheese-stuffed pineapple stand at room temperature for 15 minutes to soften before serving. Place on serving plate and surround with pineapple chunks. Spear pineapple chunks with cocktail picks and dip into cheese mixture. Makes about 2½ cups cheese dip.

PAPAYA SUNDAE

¼ cup honey
¼ cup cream
½ cup sugar
1 tablespoon butter or margarine
¼ cup lime or lemon juice

½ cup Southern-style coconut
1 papaya
1 quart vanilla ice cream
mint sprigs; stemmed cherries

The tropical taste of pineapple flavors a tangy cheese dip.

Combine honey, cream, sugar and butter. Boil 3 minutes, stirring constantly. Chill. Stir in lime juice and coconut. Halve papaya; scoop out seeds and membrane. Peel; slice crosswise, ½ inch thick. Scoop ice cream into sundae dishes and circle it with papaya slices. Pour sauce on top. Garnish with mint and cherries. (Or serve sauce at table.) Serves 6.

COLORFUL FLORIDA KEYS 3

Pigeon Key lies in the shadow of the Overseas Highway, which travels more than 100 miles out in the Gulf to reach Key West.

No romantic novel could have a plot more exciting than the real-life history of the Florida Keys, a chain of white coral islands strung in a half moon from the mainland to Key West. Like a hair-raising adventure tale, it bristles with violence and sudden death, alternating with times of peace and prosperity.

Early Spanish adventurers exploring all the way to the southernmost island found piles of human bones, presumably men slain during a battle with the fierce, near-naked Calusas. They named the place Cayo Hueso—Bone Key—which was corrupted to "Key West."

In 1513, Ponce de Leon sailed past the rocky islands and gave them a highly appropriate name, *Los Martires,* because they looked like suffering men.

Ponce de Leon claimed Florida for Spain when he came searching for gold and the Fountain of Youth. After he failed and died, followed by de Soto, the King of Spain abandoned the idea of settling Florida and moved his ships to Mexico and South America to loot them of gold, silver, jewels and precious woods.

Twice a year, these treasure-laden ships passed through the Bahama Channel and the treacherous, reef-bound water along the Keys, and brought the Keys their most despicable residents— cut-throat English pirates and French buccaneers who preyed on

27

stricken ships and attacked unwary ones, torturing and killing
crews and leaving few survivors. Thousands of ships went down.
Later, when the English won Florida, piracy continued, but
with English ships plundered by Spanish pirates. From 1812 to
1823, records show there were 3,007 piracies, about one a day!

Perhaps the most infamous of all the pirates was a huge,
fearsome former slave called Black Caesar. A myth he may be,
but not to many Keys oldtimers who contend that he lived and
plied his grisly career out of Caesar's Creek between Old Rhodes
and Elliott Keys north of Key Largo.

The Calusa Indians joined in the pirating. They were finally
destroyed by Creek Indians instructed by settlers from Georgia
to bring back slaves who had taken refuge with the Florida
Indian, and to kill Calusas. By 1765, the Calusas were gone.

Piracy did not end until 1823 when Commodore David Porter
drove the buccaneers from the Keys with a "mosquito fleet." In
1821, Spain ceded East and West Florida to the U.S. and Andrew
Jackson became territorial governor. Florida became a state in
1845.

The 1830's was a hectic boom period in Key West. Ships were
still being wrecked in the treacherous waters. Licenses were issued
giving a ship's cargo to the first salvage crew reaching it, and all
around the city, great piles of furniture, clothing, jewels and cargo
went to the highest bidder.

In 1890, Key West was the richest city per capita in the U.S.,
and had the largest population in Florida—18,000. When Federal
lighthouses stopped the wrecks, the boom was over.

Before the Civil War, when Florida seceded from the Union,
Key West remained in Union hands and fort-building began in
this Gibraltar of the Caribbean. The beautiful old handmade brick
of Fort Taylor on the island and Fort Jefferson, 60 miles west on
Dry Tortugas, are now tourists' delights.

At one time, Key West was the nation's top producer of fine
Havana cigars, before a great fire caused the plant to be moved
to Tampa's Ybor City.

A new era began for the Keys when Henry Flagler's dream
railroad spanned 128 miles of land and sea from Homestead to
Key West, and the first train arrived carrying Flagler in 1912.
One thousand school children sang a welcome; Flagler cried.

World-famed sportsmen flocked to the Keys; new towns
sprang up; new residents poured in. By 1913, Key West had

22,000 residents. Then the Labor Day hurricane of 1935 wiped out the railroad, killed hundreds, and washed out much of the one road that linked the Keys to the mainland.

Even with the building of a new Overseas Highway, prosperity did not return until World War II. By 1960, Key West had 35,956 residents, and the number keeps growing. Visitors jam the old city to see the picturesque old cedar and hardwood homes built by seafaring men, to attend Wreckers Balls and other events during the fun-filled Old Island Days in mid-winter.

Life on the Keys bred a special kind of men and women—hardy people with the valor and toughness of pioneers. A strong Cockney accent identifies many of them with the Englishmen who first left the Bahamas for the Keys to cut scarce wood and find turtles. Proudly they call themselves "Conchs" after the rose pink shellfish that is a staple in the Keys diet.

They built humble but sturdy dwellings on the white coral islands that float on the blue-green sea. And they survived on food from the sea, canned foods brought in by boat, coconuts, precious garden vegetables and fruit from the hardy little Key lime trees. Life was lonely, secluded, but they loved it.

Because there was no refrigeration, canned condensed milk was in great demand. With it, the Conchs produced a true masterpiece, Key Lime Pie.

Their fish was plentiful: crawfish (Florida lobster); stone crabs; grunt; snapper; grouper; sea trout; bonefish; mackerel; kingfish; shrimp. Great green sea turtles weighing up to 300 pounds were a major food source. But now 1971 conservation rulings protect all but the very largest and may make this delicacy scarce. However, there are still quantities of pink jumbo shrimp.

Conch foods are a fascinating blend of Southern Cracker cooking, zesty Latin, and spicy Caribbean. Conch seafood is a world away from simple New England dishes—but it is spectacularly good.

Woven into the cuisine are tropical foods such as avocado, plantain, carissa, kumquat, guava, papaya, pineapple, coconut. Many of these meld with seafood into unforgettable salads. But the most memorable dish of all is, of course, Key Lime Pie. Just be sure when you try it on the Keys, to ask for the original recipe made with sweetened condensed milk. Conchs consider this the ONLY one, and all variations as outrageous imitations.

Eat this in soup bowls with tender-crusted Cuban bread.

CRAWFISH CHELOW (Florida Lobster)

2 medium onions, chopped
6 cloves garlic, finely chopped
1 large green pepper, chopped
¼ to 1/3 cup olive oil
2 8-oz. cans tomato sauce
1 6-oz. can tomato paste

1 teaspoon salt
⅛ teaspoon pepper
3 bay leaves
¼ teaspoon oregano
4 large or 6 small crawfish

Fry onions, garlic, green pepper in oil until tender but not browned, stirring occasionally. Use enough oil to prevent scorching. Add tomato sauce and tomato paste. Rinse cans with tablespoon or two of water each and add water. Add salt, pepper, bay leaves, oregano. Remove crawfish from shells, chop in small pieces and add. Cook, uncovered, about 20 minutes, until slightly cooked down. Serve hot in soup bowls. Makes 6 servings.

Minced crawfish is similar to chelow but less soupy. It is served over white rice with black beans, green salad and Cuban bread.

MINCED CRAWFISH

½ large green pepper, chopped
½ large onion, chopped
6 small cloves garlic, finely chopped
3 tablespoons oil, bacon drippings
    or shortening
2 bay leaves

4 large or 6 small crawfish
1 8-oz. can tomato sauce
¼ teaspoon oregano
1½ teaspoons Worcestershire sauce
1 teaspoon salt
⅛ teaspoon pepper

Fry green pepper, onion and garlic in fat until tender but not browned, stirring now and then. Use more fat, if needed, to prevent scorching. Remove crawfish from shells and cut fine. Add to onion mixture with bay leaves and stir. Cook until very hot, about 3 minutes. Add tomato sauce and a little water to rinse can. Add oregano, Worcestershire sauce, salt and pepper. Cook, uncovered, about 15 minutes, until some of the liquid has cooked out. Minced crawfish should be moist but not runny with juice. Serve over fluffy hot rice. Makes 8 servings.

CONCH CHOWDER

¼ pound salt pork
2 medium onions, chopped
4 cloves garlic, crushed
1 large green pepper, chopped
1 1-pound can tomatoes
1 6-oz. can tomato paste
2 quarts hot water
1 teaspoon poultry seasoning

8 large conchs
1 tablespoon vinegar
2 teaspoons salt
½ teaspoon pepper
1 tablespoon oregano
4 bay leaves
2 tablespoons barbecue sauce
9 medium potatoes, peeled and sliced

Dice salt pork and fry in large pot. Add onions, garlic, green pepper. Cook until tender but not browned. Add tomatoes, tomato paste, hot water, poultry seasoning. Cook over low heat while preparing conch.

Pound conchs with back of knife to break up tough tissue. Chop. Add to chowder. Bring to a boil. Add vinegar, salt, pepper, oregano, bay leaves and barbecue sauce. Bring to a boil, cover, turn heat low and simmer 2 hours. Add potatoes and simmer until potatoes are tender, about 20 minutes. Makes 8 generous servings.

DOLPHIN AMANDINE

12 ½-inch thick fillets dolphin
    (about 6 ounces each)
1 teaspoon salt
⅛ teaspoon white pepper

1 to 1½ teaspoons paprika
½ cup (1 stick) butter
1 6-oz. package slivered almonds

Place dolphin fillets in a lightly oiled shallow pan. No rack is needed. Sprinkle with salt, pepper and paprika. Cook 1 minute in center of electric oven, then 6 to 7 minutes close under broiler. In gas oven, cook 1 minute in upper part of oven, 6 to 7 minutes under broiler flame.

Meanwhile, melt butter. Add almonds and cook over very low heat about 5 minutes, until pale brown. Pour over hot dolphin and serve at once. Makes 12 servings.

OCEAN REEF GROUPER CHOWDER

1 fresh grouper, about 5 pounds
1 gallon water
1 tablespoon salt
1 large onion, coarsely chopped
4 whole cloves
1 bay leaf
1 large stalk celery, chopped
1 stick butter

1 medium onion, finely chopped
1 teaspoon curry powder
½ teaspoon rosemary
½ teaspoon oregano
½ teaspoon leaf thyme
1½ cups flour
2 teaspoons monosodium glutamate
Light cream, about 1 quart

Clean grouper and cut off head. Place grouper with head in large kettle with water, salt, large onion, cloves, bay leaf and celery. Bring to a boil, reduce heat to a boil, reduce heat to simmer and cook about 12 minutes, or until fish flakes when pierced with fork. Take pot off the heat; strain liquid. Remove fish from bones and cut in bite-size pieces. Saute onion in butter in a saucepan until tender but not brown. Add curry powder, rosemary, oregano, thyme and flour, stirring smooth. Stir in stock drained from grouper and monosodium glutamate. Stir until smooth then reduce to simmer and cook 20 to 25 minutes.

Using 1/3 as much cream as fish liquid, bring cream to boil in a separate pan. Pour into chowder; add grouper chunks. Reheat; serve at once. Makes 20 servings—enough for a chowder party. (Tip: freeze leftover chowder and reheat, but do not boil.)

BAKED MACKEREL IN SPANISH SAUCE

1 3-pound King or Spanish Mackerel
cooking oil
salt and pepper
½ cup tomato juice

1 tablespoon onion, finely chopped
1 cup Spanish Sauce
¼ cup bread crumbs
2 tablespoons butter

Clean fish, rub with cooking oil or fat and season with salt and pepper. In oiled pan, place fish, pour on tomato juice; sprinkle with onion. Bake at 350 degrees F. about 30 minutes, basting occasionally. Remove from oven; pour Spanish Sauce over fish, sprinkle top with bread crumbs and dot with butter. Place in oven until browned.

Key West families of Spanish origin use garlic freely, which must be done for authentic flavor. You may, of course, reduce it to suit your taste.

SPANISH SAUCE

2 green peppers, coarsely chopped
5 cloves garlic, chopped finely
½ cup fresh, light olive oil
3 onions, coarsely chopped
1 1-pound 12-oz. can tomatoes
1 10½ oz. can tomato puree

2 bay leaves
¼ teaspoon oregano
1½ teaspoons Worcestershire sauce
juice of 1 lime
salt and pepper

In saucepan, heat olive oil and cook garlic and green peppers until latter are almost tender. Add onion; cook until tender but not browned. Stir in tomatoes, tomato puree, bay leaves, oregano, Worcestershire sauce, lime juice and salt and pepper to taste. Simmer until slightly thickened and well blended, about 20 minutes, stirring occasionally. Makes about 2½ cups sauce.

KEY WEST PAELLA

½ cup olive oil
4 cloves garlic
2 bay leaves
1 teaspoon oregano
2 pounds chicken pieces
½ pound diced pork loin
1 cup chopped onion
1 chorizo (hot Spanish sausage)
½ cup diced cooked ham
4 raw oysters
4 raw clams

8 raw shrimp, peeled and de-veined
1 cup long grain rice
4 cups hot stock or water
1½ teaspoons salt
¼ teaspoon pepper
1 teaspoon monosodium glutamate
¼ teaspoon powdered saffron
1 large green pepper, sliced
2 or 3 pimientos, halved
1 8-oz. can peas, drained
Optional Garnish: Hard cooked eggs, asparagus

Heat olive oil in paella (the casserole); saute garlic and bay leaves gently 3 minutes. Remove; add oregano, chicken and pork to oil and cook, turning until browned and almost done. Add onion, sausage cut in inch pieces, and ham. Saute 3 minutes. Add oysters, clams, shrimp, rice, stock, salt, pepper, monosodium glutamate and saffron. (To use thread saffron, crush and heat in spoon of water over pot for a minute or two, then add.) Boil for 10 minutes. Arrange green pepper, pimientos and peas on top for decoration. Cover and bake in moderate 375 deg. oven for 15 minutes. Makes 6 to 8 servings.

POMPANO STEW

½ pound white bacon
2 medium onions, chopped
3 tomatoes, peeled and chopped
1 clove garlic
1 small green pepper, chopped
1 cup celery, chopped

4 medium potatoes, peeled and diced
1½ quarts water
3 pounds pompano cut in steaks
1 teaspoon salt
⅛ teaspoon pepper
2 tablespoons flour

Dice white bacon and fry. Add onions, tomatoes, garlic, green pepper and celery. Cook until tender, stirring occasionally. Add potatoes and water. Cover; cook until potatoes are tender. Add pompano, salt and pepper, and steam until tender, 10 to 15 minutes. Stir flour to smooth paste with a little water. Stir into broth, cooking and stirring until thick and smooth. Makes 5 to 6 servings.

For superb taste, use fresh Florida shrimp. If frozen shrimp are used, thaw before using. Shell, de-vein, bread and refrigerate shrimp until chilled. (Tip: Cooking oil won't get too salty and can be re-used if shrimp are salted after cooking.)

FRIED FLORIDA SHRIMP

1 pound Florida shrimp, cleaned
¼ cup flour
¼ cup undiluted evaporated milk

½ cup fine dry bread crumbs
salt, pepper to taste

Shell, de-vein shrimp. Shake in flour placed in small paper bag. Dip into milk, drain slightly then coat with bread crumbs. Pat on until breading sticks firmly. Refrigerate. Fry in 350 deg. deep fat until golden brown, about 3 minutes. Season with salt and pepper; serve at once. Makes 3 big servings.

SHRIMP COCKTAIL

To prepare boiled shrimp, wash shrimp in shells under cold running water. Drop into COLD water, allowing 1 tablespoon salt to each quart water. When water boils, add a tablespoon of vinegar. Time from moment boiling starts, and boil shrimp just 2 minutes, no longer. Drain and remove shells; de-vein. (Tip: Beware of overcooking. It makes shrimp tough.)

COCKTAIL SAUCE

½ cup tomato catsup
6 tablespoons lemon or lime juice
⅛ teaspoon salt
1 tablespoon grated horseradish

3 drops Tabasco sauce
½ teaspoon celery salt
lettuce leaves

Blend all ingredients except lettuce; chill in refrigerator. Line cocktail glasses with lettuce, fill with chilled cooked shrimp and sauce. Makes 4 servings.

Pompano is considered Florida's "fish de luxe." The flesh is delicate and especially fine flavored.

POMPANO AMANDINE

1 1-to to 1½-pound pompano
about ½ stick butter
¼ teaspoon salt

dash white pepper
2 tablespoons slivered almonds
lime wedges; parsley

Clean pompano, but leave whole with head on. Melt butter in small skillet, using enough to measure ¼ inch deep in pan. Saute fish until it flakes easily, 5 to 6 minutes on each side. Remove pompano to warmed serving dish; season with salt and pepper. In pan drippings, cook almonds until just pale golden. Pour butter-almond sauce over pompano. Garnish with lime and parsley. Makes 1 serving.

Coconut delicacies are as traditional to Key West as widow's walks and Martello Towers. Fresh coconut cake is a Key West trademark. It was served to former President Truman, the late President Eisenhower, the late Secretary of State John Foster Dulles and countless other dignitaries who visited the island. Old-timers insist that freshly grated coconut must be used. One meltingly good taste and you know how right they are! (Tip: But frozen grated coconut is the next best thing.)

KEY WEST COCONUT CAKE

¾ cup shortening	½ teaspoon salt
1½ cups sugar	1 cup coconut milk
3 cups cake flour	1 teaspoon vanilla extract
4 teaspoons baking powder	5 egg whites

Cream together shortening and sugar. Sift together flour, baking powder and salt. Add alternately with milk to creamed mixture. Add vanilla extract. Beat egg whites stiff; fold in. Pour into 2 oiled 8x8x2-inch layer pans or 2 oiled 9-inch layer pans. Bake in moderate 375 deg. oven 30 minutes. Cool 5 minutes. Remove layers from pans; cool on wire rack. When cool, fill and frost.

COCONUT FILLING

2 egg whites	½ teaspoon salt
1½ cups sugar	1 teaspoon vanilla extract
½ cup coconut milk	1 coconut, grated
1 tablespoon white corn syrup	

Combine all ingredients except vanilla and coconut. With electric mixer, beat at high speed about 1 minute to blend. Then place over rapidly boiling water, using mixer to beat continuously until firm peaks form—about 8 minutes. Remove from heat, turn into bowl and add vanilla extract. Fill and frost cooled cake layers, sprinkling generously with grated coconut.

MISCELLANEOUS RECIPES

COCONUT CHICKEN SALAD

1 cup chopped cooked chicken	salt to taste
1 cup diced celery	½ cup mayonnaise thinned with a
½ cup grated coconut	little cream
½ cup green seedless grapes	1 ripe avocado
¼ cup chopped pecans or walnuts	

Prepare chicken, celery, coconut, grapes, nuts. Add salt; mix with mayonnaise. Chill. Cut avocado in half; rub lime on fruit to prevent darkening. When ready to serve, fill with chicken salad. Makes 2 servings.

GUACAMOLE

2 ripe avocadoes	4 drops red hot sauce
juice of 1 lime	½ of 3-oz. package cream cheese
½ teaspoon salt	1 tablespoon minced pimiento
½ teaspoon chili powder	(optional)
2 teaspoons fresh onion juice	

Peel avocadoes, remove pits and mash with silver fork to prevent darkening. Add lime juice then blend in seasonings and cream cheese. If pimiento is used, stir it in last. Use as a dip with potato chips or stuff tomatoes for salad. (Tip: If guacamole must stand for some time, place in refrigerator with pit in center and it will not darken.)

COCONUT COOKIE BALLS

2 egg whites	2 cups grated coconut
1 cup sugar	1 teaspoon vanilla extract
1 tablespoon flour	

Beat egg whites stiff. Beat in sugar, a little at a time, then beat in flour. Blend in coconut and vanilla. Drop by teaspoons onto well-greased cookie sheet. Bake in 350 deg. moderate oven about 18 minutes or until lightly browned. Remove from pan at once. Makes about 30 cookies.

CARIBBEAN GUAVA PUNCH

2 quarts Jamaica rum	2 quarts water
1½ cups Key Lime juice	1 pound guava jelly
2¼ pounds sugar	½ pint brandy
2 quarts strong tea	3 quarts ginger ale
1 quart sweet sherry	

Mix all ingredients in large punch bowl, well iced. Just before serving time, add ginger ale.

This potent mixture is a great favorite on the Florida Keys. Natives like it on seafood cocktail, seafood salad, or broiled, baked or fried fish.

LIME SOUR

Strain 1 cup lime juice into a bottle. Add 1 tablespoon salt and cork tightly. Let stand at room temperature until fermented—two to four weeks.

The Key Lime Pie orginated by pioneer settlers of the Florida Keys has gained worldwide recognition. Here is the original recipe, plus two delicious variations.

THE ORIGINAL KEY LIME PIE

6 egg yolks, beaten slightly	1 9-inch baked pie shell, pastry or
1 15-ounce can sweetened condensed	crumb
milk	6 egg whites, stiffly beaten
½ cup Key Lime juice (or Persian	4 tablespoons sugar
Lime)	

Combine egg yolks and condensed milk. Mix well. Add lime juice; blend well. Turn into baked pie shell. Beat egg whites until stiff peaks form, gradually adding sugar. Swirl onto pie, spreading to edge of pie shell all around. Bake in 300 degree oven until meringue is pale honey-colored.

LIME CHIFFON PIE

1 envelope unflavored gelatin	¼ teaspoon salt
¼ cup cold water	green food coloring
3 eggs, separated	1 teaspoon grated lemon peel
1 cup sugar, divided	1 cup heavy whipped cream
½ cup lime juice	1 baked 9-inch pie shell

Soften gelatin in cold water. In top of double boiler, beat egg yolks slightly. Add 2/3 cup sugar, lime juice and salt. Cook over hot water until thick, stirring constantly; remove from heat. Stir in softened gelatin until thoroughly dissolved. Tint pale green with food coloring. Chill until slightly thickened. Beat egg whites until stiff but not dry. Gradually beat in remaining 1/3 cup sugar and grated lemon peel. Fold into gelatin mixture, then fold in half of whipped cream. Pile into cooled pie shell; chill until firm. Swirl remaining whipped cream onto top of pie. Refrigerate until served.

A pirate parrot watches over gold doubloons and Lime Chiffon Pie.

FROZEN LIME PIE

½ cup Key Lime or Persian Lime juice
1 15-oz. can sweetened condensed milk
5 egg whites
2 tablespoons sugar
1 tablespoon grated lemon rind
few drops green food color
1 9-inch graham cracker pie shell

Combine lime juice and condensed milk, stirring until thick and smooth. Beat egg whites until foamy. Add sugar, one tablespoon at a time, and continue beating until stiff. Add food color. Fold in lime-milk mixture. Sprinkle lemon rind on bottom of pie shell; turn filling into shell. Chill until set. Freeze and keep until time to serve or serve without freezing. For topping, swirl on sweetened whipped cream.

A sauce in the Keys tradition, great over Jello or ice cream.

TROPICAL DESSERT SAUCE

1 can evaporated milk
2/3 cup sugar
½ teaspoon almond extract
juice of 2 Key Limes

Chill milk; beat with electric mixer until foamy. Add sugar; whip again. Squeeze limes, strain juice. Add almond extract and juice. Tangy but sweet, this has the consistency of whipped cream. Makes 1 cup.

The British influence is evident in this rich pudding, brought to Key West from the Bahama Islands.

QUEEN OF ALL PUDDINGS

1 quart milk, scalded	½ cup guava jelly
2 cups soft bread crumbs	3 egg whites
3 egg yolks	6 tablespoons sugar
¾ cup sugar	flaked coconut
2 tablespoons butter	

Pour scalded milk over bread crumbs; cool. Beat egg yolks lightly with ¾ cup sugar, add to milk and bread crumbs. Melt butter in a deep baking dish. Add butter to custard, then pour custard into baking dish. Preheat oven to 350 deg.; place pudding in oven in pan of warm water. Bake 1 hour 15 minutes, or until silver knife inserted in center comes out clean. When pudding has set, remove from oven and spread top with guava jelly. Beat egg whites until foamy, gradually adding sugar until peaks form. Swirl on top; sprinkle with coconut. Bake in 350 deg. oven 12 to 15 minutes, until lightly browned.

A seaside dinner of succulent Florida seafood and Key Lime Pie.

Spanish pirates once rode the waves where now a peaceful sailboat regatta drifts across Tampa Bay off St. Petersburg.

Tampa is the name of the Indian town shown on 1580 maps. Fifty-two years before that Narvaez, commissioned governor of Florida, took a party of men inland to explore. He was followed in 1539 by de Soto, who came ashore and conquered the local Indians.

The first American settlement was a log fort built in 1823. By the time of the War Between the States, Tampa's vast pastures were filled with cattle and there was brisk trade with Cuba.

When four companies moved out to join the Confederate Army, the defenseless town was blockaded and shelled in 1863 and later occupied by Federal forces. The city was in desperate condition after the war when yellow fever swept through the area.

Progress did not really begin until 1889, when the railroad reached Tampa. Phosphate was discovered and a lively industry sprang up. Ybor brought his cigar factory and thousands of workers. And Henry Plant built the huge Tampa Bay Hotel, hoping to outdo Henry Flagler's east coast success. This became troop headquarters during the Spanish American War and Col. Theodore Roosevelt trained his Rough Riders in the hotel's backyard.

There was another great epidemic, this time of typhoid fever, and troops were tended by Clara Barton, founder of Red Cross.

After the war's end, Tampa again thrived. This became the capital of the world for production of high class, handmade Havana cigars. The boom period saw hotels and apartments built, also the Gandy Bridge which spanned Tampa Bay and connected the city with St. Petersburg.

The fine natural port made it a natural spot for concentrated action during World War II, and shipbuilding gave jobs to thousands. Another aid to community growth was MacDill Air Force Base.

In the 70's, the Tampa area has really come into its own, with growth in clean space-age industry. And it has an airport that is one of the nation's finest, just a short pleasant drive from Orlando's incomparable Disney World. It's worth the drive just to see the spectacular Skyway Bridge linking Tampa and St. Petersburg with South Florida.

Florida's lower Gulf Coast bustles, but in a relaxed sort of way. Whoever they are—prosperous orange grove men, young industrialists, retired citizens, taxi-drivers—the people take time to flash a smile and pass the time of day.

From Fort Myers to Tarpon Springs, it is a land of white sugar beaches and lazy rivers that join streams with the blue Gulf; of shadowy art museums and colorful circus quarters; of picturesque sponge fishing boats and bird sanctuaries.

Each February, Tampa surrenders to fun in the form of swashbuckling "pirates" who re-invade the city via a full-rigged pirate ship during the annual Gasparilla Festival. This duplicates the invasion of Jose Gaspar, a nineteenth century buccaneer.

But to many people, the most memorable thing about Tampa or the West Coast is one incomparable masterpiece—yard-long Cuban bread, crusty beige outside, 36 inches of delicate white fluff inside.

Southern food is still king in Tampa, prepared by talented cooks both White and Black. But space age industry is bringing a cross-section of America to the area and the cookery is growing more cosmopolitan.

Of course, Ybor City's Spanish restaurants—among the nation's best—have lent a Latin flavor to local menus. Party fare is likely to include Garbanzo Bean Soup as well as fruit cake, Arroz con Pollo as well as Dixie Coconut Cake.

Agriculture is big business, providing plenty of locally produced citrus and beef, garden vegetables, guavas, watermelons and
berries. Fish are plentiful along the coast and local cooks do great
things with shrimp and crabment, lobster and fish.

In 1905, 25 miles northwest of Tampa, Tarpon Springs was
born. This Greek community was settled by sponge fishermen
lured from their homeland to the bountiful west coast sponge beds.

In colorful ceremonies, the sponge fleet is blessed each Jan. 6
and young men dive for the golden cross flung into the bay by the
archbishop. Even more exciting is the local Greek food—savory,
herb-blessed lamb, sweet stone crab claws, and a salad that is a
work of art.

YBOR CITY SPECIALTIES

TENDER CRUST CUBAN BREAD

1½ package active dry yeast
2-2/3 cups warm water
1¼ tablespoons salt
1¼ tablespoons sugar

8 cups sifted all-purpose flour
¼ cup yellow corn meal
¼ cup melted butter or margarine

Dissolve yeast in 2/3 cup warm water until soft. Add salt, sugar and remaining 2 cups warm water, stirring thoroughly. Add flour a cup at a time, beating
it in with a wooden spoon. Working on a lightly floured board, knead dough for
about 15 minutes, until it is smooth and elastic. Place in a well-oiled, large bowl,
brush top with melted butter and cover with tea towel. Set in a warm place for
about one hour, until dough doubles in size. Punch dough down with your fist.
Again on lightly floured board, shape dough into two long, narrow loaves. Sprinkle
cookie sheet with corn meal and place loaves on it. Cut several slashes in top. Let
rise 5 minutes. Brush tops with melted butter and place in cold oven. Turn oven
to 400 deg. F. and bake 45 minutes or until loaves are golden brown. Place pan
of boiling water in oven during baking time. Remove bread from oven, again
brush with melted butter. Makes 2 loaves, golden crusted outside, light and snowy
inside.

SPANISH BEAN SOUP
(from famous Columbia Restaurant)

½ pound dried garbanzo beans
10 cups water
1 tablespoon salt
1 beef bone
1 ham bone
2 quarts water
¼ pound salt pork, chopped fine

pinch paprika
1 tablespoon shortening
1 chopped onion
1 pound potatoes, peeled and quartered
1 pinch saffron
1 chorizo Spanish sausage cut in thin
  slices

In large pot, place beans in salted water to soak overnight. Next day, drain
water and place beans, beef and ham bones and 2 quarts water in large pot. Place
over low heat; simmer 45 minutes. Fry the chopped salt pork, add paprika and
onion (plus 1 tablespoon shortening if needed) and cook until onion is tender.
Add to beans, then add potatoes. Toast saffron on the cover of a casserole or in

Chicken and Yellow Rice Valenciana is an Ybor City specialty.

the oven and mash before measuring. Mix with a little hot stock from the pot and add to soup. Taste and season with salt and pepper. In about 15 minutes, when potatoes are done, put chorizo slices in soup and serve hot. Serves 4.

FLORIDA MULLET WITH SPANISH SAUCE

1 3-pound fresh water mullet (or
    red snapper)
salt and pepper
flour
6 tablespoons melted butter
¼ cup chopped onion
2 cups chopped celery
¼ cup chopped green pepper
3 cups canned tomatoes

1 teaspoon Worcestershire sauce
1 tablespoon catsup
½ teaspoon chili powder
½ lemon, thinly sliced
1 bay leaf
1 clove minced garlic
1 teaspoon salt
2 teaspoons sugar
dash cayenne pepper

Mix flour, salt and pepper and coat mullet inside and out. Melt butter in skillet and over low heat, cook onion, celery and green pepper for 15 minutes. Add all remaining ingredients and simmer until celery is tender. Press mixture through potato ricer; pour sauce over cleaned fish and bake in 350 deg. oven 45 minutes, basting frequently with Spanish sauce. Serves 4 generously.

CHICKEN AND YELLOW RICE VALENCIANA

1 2½-lb. frying chicken, quartered
½ cup fresh olive oil
2 chopped onions
1 chopped green pepper
1 clove garlic, chopped fine
1 bay leaf
2 tablespoons salt
1 small can tomatoes, drained
¼ teaspoon pepper

2½ cups rice
5 cups water + 2 chicken bouillon
    cubes
½ cup sherry wine (optional)
⅛ teaspoon saffron
1 cup green peas
1 small can pimientos
1 doz. green olives

Brown chicken in olive oil over medium heat. Add onions, green pepper and garlic. Continue cooking until slightly brown, about 5 minutes. Return chicken to pot and stir in salt, bay leaf, tomatoes, pepper. Add rice, water in which 2 chicken bouillon cubes have been dissolved, and wine. Dissolve saffron in small amount of water and add (or use a few drops of yellow food color mixed with water). Bring to boil. Bake in preheated oven at 350 deg. 20 minutes. Garnish with green peas, olives and pimientos. Makes 4 servings.

GREEK DISHES

LOUIS PAPPAS' FAMOUS GREEK SALAD

Make a potato salad from these ingredients:

6 boiling potatoes	½ cup thinly sliced green onion
2 medium onions	½ cup salad dressing
¼ cup finely chopped parsley	salt

Salad ingredients:

1 large head lettuce	4 slices canned cooked beets
3 cups potato salad	4 peeled, cooked shrimp
12 sprigs watercress	4 anchovy fillets
2 tomatoes cut into 6 wedges each	12 black Greek olives
1 peeled cucumber cut into 8 long fingers	4 radishes cut like roses
	4 whole green onions
1 peeled avocado cut into wedges	½ cup distilled white vinegar
4 portions of Feta (Greek cheese)	¼ cup each olive and salad oil, blended
1 green pepper cut into 8 rings	oregano

Save 10 outside lettuce leaves and shred remaining lettuce finely. Prepare all vegetables as indicated above. On large platter, place whole lettuce leaves, 3 cups potato salad mounted in center and covered with shredded lettuce then with watercress. Alternate tomato wedges and cucumber fingers around outside of platter; circle with avocado slices. Atop the salad, arrange the slices of Feta cheese, green pepper slices, olives, peppers, green onions. Finally, top salad with slices of beets, shrimp and anchovy filets. Sprinkle with vinegar and blended oil then with oregano. Serve at once with garlic toasted Greek bread. (Served at Louis Pappas Restaurant in Tarpon Springs, Fla., this is called a salad for 4.)

MOUSAKA POTATOES WITH BEEF

½ clove garlic, chopped	pinch cinnamon
½ cup oil for frying (olive oil)	pinch sugar
6-8 medium potatoes, sliced	1 cup water
1 large onion, chopped	¼ cup dry red wine
1 pound ground beef (or lamb)	2 cans hot tomato sauce
1 teaspoon salt	2 bay leaves
¼ teaspoon pepper	

Lightly brown garlic in oil; remove. Saute potatoes in oil until light brown but not done. Set potatoes aside. Mix meat, onion, garlic, salt and pepper to taste. Fry for 3 minutes. Spread meat mixture between layers of potatoes in oiled baking dish, starting and ending with potatoes. Combine wine, water, tomato sauce, cinnamon and sugar. Place bay leaves atop casserole and pour over all the wine liquid. Bake in 350 deg. oven 45 to 60 minutes. Remove bay leaves before serving hot. Serves 6.

LAMB KEBOBS, GREEK STYLE

½ teaspoon Tabasco
½ cup olive or salad oil
¼ cup lime or lemon juice
¼ cup red wine, optional
1 tablespoon onion juice
1 teaspoon dry mustard
½ teaspoon salt

⅛ teaspoon basil
⅛ teaspoon thyme
2 pounds boneless lamb shoulder cut in
    1½-inch cubes
1 green pepper cut in 1 inch pieces
3 tomatoes, quartered
12 small whole onions

Blend Tabasco, oil, lime juice, wine and onion juice in bowl. Add dry mustard, salt, basil and thyme. Add meat cubes. (Beef chuck may be substituted, but if used should be sprinkled with meat tenderizer.) Let stand 5 hours or overnight. Alternate meat and vegetables on skewers. Place in pre-heated broiler or on grill about 4 inches from heat. Broil approximately 10 minutes on each side. Serve with rice pilaf. Makes 6 servings.

Basil and thyme add zest to Lamb Kebobs, Greek Style.

DIXIE COCONUT CAKE
(Coconut is baked in the cake layers and used in frosting.)

3 cups sifted cake flour
2 teaspoons double acting baking
    powder
½ teaspoon salt
½ cup butter

1½ cups sugar
1 cup coconut, Premium Shred
1 cup water
1½ teaspoons lemon extract
4 egg whites, stiffly beaten

Sift flour once, measure, add baking powder and salt; sift twice more. Cream butter until smooth, gradually adding sugar and creaming until soft and fluffy. To this, add coconut, then flour, then water, a little each time, beating well after each addition. When batter is smooth, stir in lemon extract; fold in egg whites which should be quite stiff. Bake in 2 greased loaf pans 8x4x3 inches at 350 deg. 1 hour and 15 minutes. Frost top and sides with Coconut 7-Minute Frosting.

COCONUT 7-MINUTE FROSTING

2 unbeaten egg whites
1½ cups sugar
5 tablespoons cold water

1½ teaspoons light corn syrup
1 teaspoon vanilla
1 cup lightly toasted coconut

In upper double boiler, combine egg whites, sugar, water and corn syrup; beat with rotary egg beater until well mixed. Place over rapidly boiling water and continue beating. Cook 7 minutes or until frosting stands in peaks. Remove from heat, add vanilla, beat until thick enough to spread. Sprinkle with toasted coconut. Makes enough to frost 2 cakes, top and sides.

HOT WINE ORANGE PUNCH

juice of 1 orange
¾ pint water

½ pound sugar
1 bottle red wine

In one saucepan, heat water and half of juice squeezed from orange. In another pan, dissolve sugar with remaining juice. Combine; boil 10 minutes. Heat red wine till it bubbles; pour in the other mixture. Serve hot with thin slices of orange floating on top. A stimulating cold weather drink!

GREEK HONEY CAKES (Melomacarona)

2 cups salad oil
¼ pound butter
½ cup sugar
½ cup orange juice
5 cups sifted flour
3 teaspoons baking powder
¼ cup water

1 cup finely chopped walnuts
½ teaspoon cinnamon
⅛ teaspoon ground cloves
⅛ cup rum
1 pound honey
½ cup warm water
½ cup finely chopped walnuts

Stir until blended oil, butter and sugar; stir in orange juice then flour and mix till smooth. Quickly mix baking powder with ¼ cup water and stir at once into dough. Mix in 1 cup walnuts, cinnamon and cloves. Shape dough into cakes 3x1x½-inch. Bake on ungreased cookie sheet in 350 deg. oven 20 to 25 minutes. Cool on wire rack. Warm honey and mix with ¼ cup warm water. Dip cool cakes into honey, sprinkle with chopped walnuts and drain on rack over waxed paper. Makes about 24.

MARSHMALLOW FUDGE CAKE
(A novel filling—and so easy to do!)

2-2/3 cups sifted cake flour
3½ teaspoons baking powder
½ teaspoon salt
2 cups sugar
1/3 cup salad oil

2 eggs
1 cup milk
1 teaspoon vanilla
2 ounces unsweetened chocolate, melted
16 marshmallows

Sift together twice flour, baking powder, salt and sugar. Add oil, eggs, milk, vanilla and chocolate; blend well then beat 2 minutes. Pour into two 8-inch square pans, greased and lined with brown paper. Bake in 325 deg. oven 1 hour. Cool. Place marshmallows atop one layer and broil to lightly brown. Cool 15 minutes. Top with plain cake layer and cover with Fudge Frosting.

QUICK CARAMEL CAKE
(A modern version with baked-on topping)

2 cups cake flour
3 teaspoons baking powder
1 teaspoon salt
1¼ cups sugar
½ cup shortening (use one recom-
    mended for quick cakes)
¾ cup milk

1½ teaspoons vanilla
2 eggs
TOPPING:
2 egg whites
1 cup brown sugar
½ cup chopped pecans

Let all ingredients stand at room temperature 45 minutes before use. To sifted flour, add baking powder, salt, sugar; sift again into large mixer bowl. Add shortening, milk, vanilla. Beat 2 minutes with mixer at low speed. Add unbeaten eggs and beat 1 minute longer. Pour into greased 8½x13½-inch pan. Set aside. Clean mixer beaters and beat egg whites till stiff but not dry. Gradually add brown sugar; beat well. Spread atop cake; sprinkle with nuts and bake on center shelf in 350 deg. oven 35 minutes.

PINEAPPLE DROP COOKIES

1 cup light brown sugar
½ cup shortening mixed with butter
1 unbeaten egg
1 teaspoon vanilla
¾ cup crushed pineapple
2 cups sifted all-purpose flour

1 teaspoon baking powder
½ teaspoon salt
½ teaspoon soda
¾ cup chopped walnuts
½ cup raisins

Heat oven to 375 deg. Stir together sugar, shortening, egg and vanilla till blended. Spoon pineapple from can with as little syrup as possible into measuring cup and add. Stir in sifted dry ingredients, then walnuts and raisins. Drop by heaping teaspoonfuls on ungreased cookie sheet. Bake at 375 deg. for 12 minutes till lightly browned. Makes 36.

FLORIDA FRUIT CAKE

1 cup salad oil
1½ cups brown sugar
4 eggs
3 cups sifted flour
1 teaspoon baking powder
2 teaspoons salt

1 teaspoon cloves
1 cup orange juice
1 cup chopped candied pineapple
2 cups candied cherries, halved
1½ cups seedless raisins
1 cup chopped dates
2 tablespoons peach brandy

In large bowl, beat oil, sugar and eggs 2 minutes. Sift together 2 cups of flour with baking powder, salt and spices. Stir into oil mixture with orange juice. Mix remaining cup of flour with fruits and nuts. Combine with batter and mix thoroughly. Pour batter into two 9x5-inch loaf pans lined with greased brown paper. Bake in 275 deg. oven 2½ to 3 hours. Remove and cool. Sprinkle 2 tablespoons brandy over cake, wrap and store in cool place. If desired, decorate with candied pineapple and cherries.

ORANGE RUM CREAM CAKE

1¾ cups sifted cake flour	1 cup sugar
1 tablespoon baking powder	8 beaten egg yolks
¼ teaspoon salt	1 teaspoon grated orange rind
½ cup shortening	½ cup milk

Have all ingredients at room temperature. Sift together twice flour, baking powder and salt. Cream shortening till fluffy; gradually add sugar. Blend till mixture is creamy. Stir in egg yolks and orange rind until well mixed. Alternately add dry ingredients and milk, beating after each addition. Turn into two greased 8-inch cake pans and bake in 350 deg. oven 30 minutes. Cool 10 minutes; turn onto cake rack. Fill with Orange-Rum Filling and frost with whipped cream.

ORANGE RUM FILLING: Cream 3 tablespoons butter with ¾ teaspoon grated orange rind. Gradually add ½ cup sifted confectioners sugar, blending after each addition. Add dash of salt; mix well. Add 1 cup more confectioners sugar alternately with 2 tablespoons orange juice, beating till smooth after each addition. Blend in 1 teaspoon rum. Spread on cake layer.

LIME PUDDING CAKE
(Crusty cake topping above, rich lime sauce beneath)

2 eggs, separated	3 tablespoons flour
¾ cup sugar	¼ teaspoon salt
3 tablespoons lime juice	1 cup milk
1 teaspoon grated lime rind	

Beat egg whites, gradually adding ½ cup sugar, until stiff and glossy. Set aside. Beat egg yolks. Add lime juice and grated rind to egg yolks. Mix sugar, flour and salt together. Sprinkle over lime mixture and beat well. Add milk; blend well. Fold egg yolk mixture into beaten egg whites. Pour into 6 greased custard cups. Set in shallow pan of water and bake in 350 deg. oven 35 minutes until firm. Serves 6.

THE HEARTLAND

Spanish explorers never found gold in Florida, but they brought citrus — Florida's richest treasure.

Just a few hours by car takes you far from the glamour of the Gold Coast into Florida's quietly beautiful heartland, a world of beef cattle ranches, orange groves and vegetable farms. To the north in Ocala, racing thoroughbreds are raised on the rolling green hills.

Around Lake Okeechobee, rich black mucklands have been producing sugar cane in volume since 1929. The industry, centered in Clewiston, became a giant when Castro's Cuba was cut out of the American market and Florida sugar cane became a prime supplier of the nation's needs.

In this same region, and on farms as far south as Homestead south of Miami, much of the nation's supply of winter vegetables are grown. The two large Seminole Indian Reservations are near the lake—Big Cypress 30 miles east of Immokalee and Brighton—35,660 acres on the northwest shore of Lake Okeechobee.

The Indians are hard-working cowboys whose herds of beef cattle are steadily being improved. But other ranchers account for most of the more than 75 percent of Florida's beef cattle which are produced in central and south central areas, especially in Polk, Osceola, Hendry, Highlands, Hardee, DeSoto, Hillsborough, Okeechobee and Glades counties.

From Punta Gorda to Kissimmee, cattle graze on the flat prairies. Levis, ten-gallon hats and boots are the uniform of the day and rodeos feature exciting riding and roping in the true western tradition.

Kissimmee—called Cow Town—had the dubious honor of originating the first bar for drinking men who did not want to get off their horses to drink. The ride-in bar was begun about 1870, ten years before the west adopted the idea.

Spanish explorers brought cattle into the state and their runaways turned wild, then were herded by the Indians. During the second Spanish occupation of Florida, from 1813 to 1821, the Spanish gave land grants to homesteaders who stocked the ranges with cattle from Europe as well as herds driven down from the southern states. As the Seminoles retreated into the Everglades, cattle ranchers moved in behind them all along the Kissimmee Valley.

White "humpbacked" Brahman cows were introduced because of their hardiness, resistance to insects, disease, heat, and ability to live off sparse grasslands. Especially in recent years, they have been improved by crossbreeding with Black Angus, Hereford, Santa Gertrudis and others, but the trend is now toward more purebred cattle other than the Brahman.

By 1895, when Frederic Remington, the noted writer-painter, visited Florida, he described the Cracker cowboys as a wild-looking group with long hair, broad-brimmed hat, and gun slung on hip. The wild west was no wilder than Florida in the nineteenth century. Cattle rustling was widespread; shoot-outs and stabbings were common. Ranchers did not venture out at night nor enter woods alone in some areas. Criminals would attack then flee deep into the Everglades' watery wilderness to hide.

At last, outraged citizens called a halt and law and order were reestablished.

Throughout the heartland, steak and chops restaurants are popular. And the cowboys' campfire victuals are much enjoyed:

fried white bacon, grits, beans, biscuits or cold corn pone, coffee boiled with the grounds until it is strong and black.

Moving north in the state, the land flows into gently rolling hills dipping down to incredibly blue lakes. And over the hills, mile on mile of orange trees march like well drilled soldiers up and over and down the hills. Ironically, the Spanish who failed in their search for gold in Florida, carried into the state the citrus seeds that were to produce its greatest treasure—oranges, grapefruit, lemons and tangerines.

Because citrus was found to have medicinal value, Columbus was under orders to carry with him seeds of the first citrus trees to reach the New World. Scattered throughout the Antilles, orange trees flourished and covered some Caribbean islands.

There are strong indications that Ponce de Leon introduced oranges to the North American mainland when he discovered Florida in 1513.

Later in 1539, Hernando de Soto planted more trees during his expedition to Florida. Spanish law required that each sailor bound for America carry one hundred seeds but because the seeds dried out, young trees were later substituted. Seminole Indians carried oranges into the Florida wilderness and today, sour orange trees thrive deep in the Everglades!

Today, the central Florida citrus belt outproduces its old rival, California, by three to one. And Florida grows more oranges than Spain, Italy and Mexico—the world's second, third and fourth place orange producers—combined! This is one of the most scenic sections of a beautiful state which far too few tourists ever glimpse.

It is a land still rich in deer, quail, doves and other game. Truck lands produce fine beans, cabbage, tomatoes, peas, cucumbers, lettuce. Honey is plentiful, as are poultry and beef, milk and eggs. Traditional Southern food is as popular as it was a hundred years ago.

But like the lofty Citrus Tower that dominates a 2000 square mile panorama of 17 million citrus trees, it is oranges that tower above all other activity in the rich heartland of Florida.

CLEWISTON FISH FRY

(Sugar is the big industry in Clewiston, and sweet-meated freshwater catfish from Lake Okeechobee hot from the frying pan, accompanied by crusty hush puppies are the favorite foods at lakeside barbecues.)

FRIED CATFISH

2 pounds skinned, pan-dressed
    catfish
1 beaten egg
2 tablespoons milk

1 cup white corn meal
2 teaspoons salt
oil for frying
parsley, lemon slices

Clean, wash and dry catfish. Dry on absorbent paper. Combine egg and milk. Mix corn meal and salt in bowl. Dip fish into egg mixture then into corn meal mixture. Heat oil to 350 deg. and fry fish until golden brown, about 8 minutes. Drain on absorbent paper. Garnish with parsley and lemon. Serve with hot hush puppies.

HUSH PUPPIES

(Old-timers say the name originated around the campfire when hunters tossed the hounds these hot breads to keep them quiet.)

2 cups corn meal
1 tablespoon flour
2 teaspoons baking powder
½ teaspoon salt
1 well beaten egg

¾ cup water
1 small onion, chopped fine
bacon grease or oil in which fish was
    fried

Sift together corn meal, flour, baking powder and salt. Mix egg, water and onion in bowl. Combine with dry ingredients and drop from a spoon into 380 deg. fat, dipping spoon first into hot fat then into butter. Fry 6 or more at a time until crisp and golden (about 1 minute), lift with slotted spoon and drain on paper towels. Serve hot with fish, or cook bite-size and serve as appetizers with beverages. Makes 20.

Holiday Fruit Compote is laced with spices and wine.

FLORIDA CITRUS RECIPES

CITRUS CHRISTMAS COMPOTE

4 Florida oranges	1 cup Marsala wine
1 papaya, fresh or canned	1 cup water
1 pineapple, fresh or canned	¾ cup sugar
2½ cups halved, pitted Ribier and	1 stick cinnamon
Emperor grapes (about ½ lb.)	3 whole cloves

Cut 3 strips orange peel from 1 orange, using vegetable peeler; reserve. Peel oranges and cut into crosswise slices. Pare papaya, cut in half lengthwise and remove seeds; cut into cubes. To prepare pineapple, cut off stem and crown ends. Cut off rind all around, from top to bottom; remove eyes with pointed knife. Cut into quarters lengthwise. Cut away core. Cut remaining meat into fingers about 2 inches long. Combine oranges, papaya, pineapple and grapes in large bowl. Combine wine, water, sugar, cinnamon stick, cloves and orange peel in saucepan; stir over medium heat until sugar dissolves. Reduce heat and simmer 5 minutes. Remove spices and peel. Cool to lukewarm. Pour syrup over fruit in bowl; cover and refrigerate 6 hours or overnight. Makes 12 servngs.

FRUIT SALAD WITH ORANGE CREAM SALAD DRESSING

1 egg	1½ tablespoons fresh lemon juice
3 tablespoons sugar	¼ cup heavy cream, whipped
¼ teaspoon salt	FRUITS FOR SALAD:
¼ teaspoon ginger	fresh orange and grapefruit sections
2 teaspoons butter	pitted grapes—pineapple chunks—
½ cup fresh orange juice	crisp salad greens

Beat egg in top of double boiler. Add sugar, salt, ginger, butter, orange juice and lemon juice; mix well. Place over boiling water and cook, stirring constantly, until mixture thickens slightly, 5 to 7 minutes. Chill. Just before serving, fold in whipped cream. Arrange fresh fruit on crisp greens; serve with dressing. Makes 1 cup, enough for 6 servings.

GRAPEFRUIT COLE SLAW

2 Florida grapefruit	½ teaspoon salt
3 cups shredded cabbage	2 teaspoons sugar
1/3 cup mayonnaise	½ teaspoon celery seed

Chill grapefruit. Cut off peel in strips from top to bottom, slicing deep enough to remove white membrane. Then cut out slices from top to bottom, removing any remaining membrane. Place sections in bowl with cabbage. Combine remaining ingredients; add to cabbage. Toss lightly. Serves 6.

BAKED STUFFED PORK CHOPS

8 1-inch rib or loin pork chops	3 cups stale ¼-inch bread cubes
salt, pepper	3 tablespoons minced onion
2 tablespoons oil	¾ teaspoon salt
1 cup finely diced celery	½ teaspoon Tabasco
1 6-oz. can frozen Florida grapefruit	1/3 cup brown sugar
concentrate, thawed and divided	

Sprinkle pork chops with salt and pepper. Brown in oil in skillet until golden brown on both sides, 15 to 20 minutes. Remove pork chops, saving 4 tablespoons of pan fat. Combine celery, ¼ cup grapefruit juice concentrate and pan fat; cook over medium heat 2 minutes. Add bread cubes, onion, salt, Tabasco; mix thoroughly. Combine remaining ½ cup grapefruit juice concentrate and brown sugar. Pour over pork chops in casserole. Arrange stuffing on top of pork chops. Bake, covered, in 350 deg. oven 30 minutes; remove cover and bake 15 minutes longer or until chops are tender. Makes 8 servings.

ORANGE SWEET POTATO CUPS

3 lbs. sweet potatoes	1 teaspoon vanilla
3 tablespoons melted butter	2 teaspoons grated orange rind
½ cup sugar	1/3 cup orange juice
1 teaspoon salt	3 Temple or Navel oranges

Boil sweet potatoes until tender; remove skins, mash and mix with all ingredients except oranges. Cut oranges in half crosswise, remove all juice and pulp but keep rind whole. Fill with hot sweet potato mixture. Place in greased baking pan and bake 30 minutes at 350 deg .F. If desired, add marshmallows and return to oven to brown. Makes 6 servings.

ORANGE MERINGUE PIE

¾ cup sugar	1 tablespoon grated orange rind
¼ cup cornstarch	1 tablespoon butter
⅛ teaspoon salt	3 egg whites
1 cup orange juice	¼ teaspoon salt
½ cup water	6 tablespoons sugar
1 tablespoon lemon juice	Baked 9-inch pie shell
3 egg yolks, slightly beaten	

Combine sugar, cornstarch and salt in medium saucepan; slowly blend in orange juice, water and lemon juice. Cook and stir over medium heat until mixture is thickened and clear. Stir a little of the hot mixture into egg yolks slowly; add to remaining mixture. Blend in orange rind and butter; mix well. Cool thoroughly. Spoon into cooled pie shell.

Beat egg whites with salt until frothy. Add sugar gradually, beating well after each addition. Continue to beat until stiff peaks form. With spoon, place mounds of meringue over filling, spreading to cover filling completely to crust. Bake in 350 deg. oven 12 to 15 minutes. Cool thoroughly.

GRAPEFRUIT AVOCADO SALAD

4 small heads Bibb lettuce	1 large purple onion, sliced thin
1 large grapefruit, peeled and sectioned	1 cup pineapple chunks
1 medium avocado, sliced lengthwise	tart French dressing

Chill all ingredients. Carefully trim out lettuce core so the head will sit flat. For each serving, place washed lettuce on plate and tuck into the leaves grapefruit sections, avocado slices, onion and pineapple chunks. Serve with tart French dressing. Makes 4 servings.

MOLASSES ORANGE BREAD

½ cup sugar
2-2/3 cups sifted all purpose flour
½ teaspoon baking soda
2 teaspoons baking powder
1½ teaspoons salt
1 cup coarsely chopped pecans

2/3 cup evaporated milk
1 tablespoon grated orange rind
½ cup orange juice
2 tablespoons salad oil
½ cup unsulphured molasses

Sift together sugar, flour, soda, baking powder and salt; add nuts. Combine evaporated milk, orange rind, orange juice, salad oil and molasses. Add to flour mixture all at once; stir just to blend. Turn into well-greased loaf pan 9x5x3 inches. Bake in 325 deg. oven 1 hour 15 minutes. Cool before removing from pan. Makes 1 loaf.

ORANGE PECAN REFRIGERATOR COOKIES

½ cup butter
1 cup sugar
¼ teaspoon salt
1 teaspoon grated orange rind
1 egg, beaten slightly
3 teaspoons baking powder

3 cups flour, sifted
¼ cup Florida orange juice
1½ cups pecan halves
1 egg white
sugar

Cream together butter, sugar and salt until light and fluffy. Add orange rind and egg. Beat thoroughly. Add baking powder to flour; sift together twice. Starting with flour mixture, add flour and orange juice to creamed mixture in 3 additions, stirring each time until well blended. Roll in wax paper and store in refrigerator overnight to chill thoroughly. Slice thin, keeping any unused dough in refrigerator as cookies bake. Place slices on an oiled cookie sheet, press pecan half on top of each cookie, and brush with unbeaten egg white. Sprinkle with sugar; bake in 375 deg. oven 10 to 12 minutes until lightly browned. Cool on racks, store in airtight cookie jar. Makes about 60.

ORANGE JUICE CAKE SURPRISE

1 large orange
½ cup sugar
1 cup raisins
¾ cup chopped walnuts
1 cup sugar
½ cup margarine

2 unbeaten eggs
1 teaspoon vanilla
2 cups sifted all-purpose flour
1 teaspoon baking soda
½ teaspoon salt
¾ cup buttermilk

Squeeze juice from orange, add ½ cup sugar, stir and set aside. Run orange peel and raisins through fine blade of food grinder, add nuts and set aside.

Using mixer, beat margarine and add 1 cup sugar, a little at a time. Beat in eggs, one at a time. Add vanilla. Sift together twice flour, soda and salt. Add alternately with buttermilk in four additions, beating smooth after each. Stir in fruit and walnuts. Turn into greased 9x9x2 pan. Bake in 350 deg. oven about 45 minutes. Cool cake in pan 5 minutes then pour orange juice mixture over it and wait 1 hour before serving warm as pudding, cold as refrigerator cake.

True traditional Southern ambrosia is simply orange sections tossed with freshly grated coconut and a bit of sugar. Marvelous though it is, this one is even more so.

HEAVENLY CREAM AMBROSIA

1 cup heavy cream, whipped
½ cup sour cream
1 tablespoon orange liqueur
2 cups orange sections

1 cup grapefruit sections
1 cup freshly grated coconut
1 cup miniature marshmallows

Whip cream then fold in sour cream and orange liqueur. Dice orange sections and grapefruit. Fold into cream with coconut and marshmallows. Chill overnight. Garnish with sliced orange steeped in orange liqueur. Serves 8.

FEATHERY LEMON-CHEESE CAKE

1 cup butter
2 cups sugar
4 eggs
3 cups sifted flour
3 teaspoons baking powder

½ teaspoon salt
1 cup milk
½ teaspoon vanilla
½ teaspoon lemon flavoring

Cream butter and sugar. Add one whole egg at a time, beating after each. Beat about 1 minute after all eggs have been added. Add dry ingredients that, have been sifted together twice, alternately adding milk thn the dry ingredients mixture. Stir in vanilla and lemon; pour into greased, floured pans and bake in 350 deg. oven 40 minutes or until done. When cool, fill with Lemon Cheese Filling.

LEMON CHEESE FILLING

1 cup sugar
4 tablespoons cornstarch, dissolved
    in a little water
juice of 2 lemons

3 tablespoons butter
2 eggs
2 egg yolks

Combine all ingredients and cook over hot water in double boiler, stirring constantly, until thick. Cool before spreading between layers. (This old-fashioned filling has no cheese in it, but the flavor and texture resembles cheese.) Cake may be sprinkled with confectioners sugar or frosted with 7-minute frosting. Or a double amount may be made, and whole cake frosted and filled with the lemon cheese mixture.

TROPICALI PUNCH

1 6-oz. can frozen limeade
    concentrate
2 6-oz. cans frozen pineapple juice
    concentrate
1 6-oz. can frozen orange juice
    concentrate

13 6-oz. cans (9¾ cups) water
2 cups superfine sugar
3 12-oz. bottles cold ginger ale
Maraschino cherries
fresh orange slices
mint sprigs

Thaw all concentrates; add sugar and water, stirring until all sugar dissolves. Place ice in large punch bowl; pour juices over ice. Just before serving time, add ginger ale, cherries, orange slices. Serve in glasses with mint sprig. Serves 30. (If desired, orange sherbet may be used in bowl instead of ice.)

CORN FRITTERS

1 cup corn, drained
2 slightly beaten eggs
1/3 cup flour
½ teaspoon baking powder

1 teaspoon salt
⅛ teaspoon pepper
2 tablespoons salad oil

Mix corn with slightly beaten eggs. Sift together flour, baking powder, salt and pepper. Combine corn and flour mixtures. Heat oil medium hot and drop fritter batter into oil. Fry until brown on bottom, turn and brown other side. Makes about 10. Serve hot.

ICED TEA PUNCH

2 tablespoons loose tea
2 cups boiling water
1 cup granulated sugar

1 cup orange juice
½ cup lemon juice
1 12 oz. bottle cold ginger ale

Pour boiling water over tea and let stand 5 minutes. Strain tea into pitcher. Add sugar; stir till dissolved. Pour in juices and chill. To serve, pour over ice in punch bowl and add ginger ale. Makes 10 cups.

TEA MARINATED FLORIDA BEEF ROAST
(Statewide winner in Florida Beef Council Contest)

Using 3 to 5 lb. Florida chuck or shoulder cut beef roast, brown well on top of stove in 2 to 3 tablespoons fat. Make enough very strong tea to cover roast ¾ way. Simmer 3 to 5 hours, until meat is fork tender. Drain off tea and place meat in baking dish. Pour half of following sauce over meat and baste several times during baking.

SAUCE

1 cup chili sauce
3 tablespoons brown sugar
juice of 2 lemons
1 tablespoon Worcestershire sauce
¼ teaspoon celery salt
1/3 cup grated onion

2 tablespoons bacon fat
1 cup water
1 teaspoon paprika
3 tablespoons vinegar
1 teaspoon salt

Combine all ingredients and stir to blend. Pour half over meat; save half. Bake uncovered at 325 deg. for 45 minutes. Serve hot sauce with meat.

BEEF CORN-PONE PIE

1 pound ground beef
1 medium onion, chopped
1 medium Bell pepper, cut in thin
    slices
3 tablespoons salad oil

1 No. 2 can tomatoes
1 No. 2 can kidney beans
salt
1 teaspoon chili powder (or to taste)

Cook onion and pepper in hot oil until onion is transparent but not brown. Add beef; cook until lightly browned. Stir in remaining ingredients; let simmer. Add chili powder just before topping with this cornbread mixture:

CORNBREAD

1½ cups corn meal
3 tablespoons flour
1 teaspoon salt
1 teaspoon soda

2 cups buttermilk
1 beaten egg
2 tablespoons bacon drippings, butter
    or margarine

Mix and sift dry ingredients. Add buttermilk and egg, stirring until well blended. Heat fat in skillet and add to batter. Turn beef mixture into iron frypan.

Mix batter well, pour over beef mixture and bake in 450 deg. oven about 25 minutes, or until golden brown.

BARBECUE BEEF LOAF

2 pounds ground beef
¾ cup milk
1½ cups soft bread crumbs
2 teaspoons salt
⅛ teaspoon pepper
1 medium carrot, grated

¼ cup diced onion
2 beaten eggs
¼ cup catsup
3 tablespoons brown sugar
2 tablespoons prepared mustard

Pour milk over bread crumbs. Add ground beef, salt, pepper, carrot, onion and beaten eggs. Mix thoroughly. Pack into 5x9-inch loaf pan. Mix together catsup, brown sugar, mustard, and spread on loaf. Bake in 300 deg. oven about 1½ hours, or until brown and done. Makes 8 servings.

SOUTHERN BARBECUE SAUCE SUPREME

1 lb. butter
1 pint apple vinegar
1 cup water
1 tablespoon dry mustard
1 large onion, grated
5 tablespoons Worcestershire sauce
2 cups tomato catsup

1 cup chili sauce
juice of 2 lemons
½ lemon left whole, seeded
1 or 2 cloves garlic, chopped and tied
      in cheesecloth bag
2 teaspoons sugar
1 bay leaf

Place all in saucepan and bring to a boil. Reduce to slow heat; simmer 30 minutes, stirring occasionally. Enough for 10 lbs. of beef, lamb or pork. Keep it warm and when meat on barbecue pit is ¾ done, swab with sauce frequently until done.

Florida's own beef is used in Flank Steak Rolls.

FLANK STEAK ROLLS

2 pounds Florida flank steak,
    cut in half
1 pound mild sausage
¼ teaspoon basil
½ teaspoon thyme
3 tablespoons bacon drippings
1 No. 2½ can tomatoes
1 6-oz. can tomato paste

1 large onion, chopped
3 teaspoons salt
¼ teaspoon pepper
1½ teaspoons chili powder
½ clove garlic
1 12-oz. package wide noodles
butter or margarine

Have butcher cut meat to half thickness. Pound steak, sprinkle with basil and thyme then spread with sausage. Roll and tie with string. Brown in hot drippings; add all remaining ingredients except noodles and butter. Cover; bring to a boil then reduce to simmer and cook slowly 1½ hours, or until meat is tender. Remove garlic. Cook noodles, drain, then place a large wedge of butter in the hot pan and turn noodles in butter until well coated. Remove string from steak roll and slice one inch thick. Serve meat with sauce atop hot noodles. Makes 6 generous servings.

PIONEER POT ROAST

¼ lb. salt pork
pepper
4 lbs. chuck roast of beef
1 clove garlic, chopped
salt
flour

4 tablespoons shortening
2 sliced onions
1 bay leaf
1 cup boiling water
1 tablespoon Worcestershire sauce

Slice salt pork thinly and sprinkle with pepper. Slash roast deeply and insert pork slices. Rub roast with garlic and salt; dredge with flour. Heat fat and brown meat well. Place in large heavy pot, place onion and bay leaf on meat and pour tin boiling water, and Worcestershire sauce. Bring to boil then reduce to simmer, place top on pot and simmer about 3 hours until meat is tender. Add more water if needed.

MOM'S SWISS STEAK

1½ lbs. round steak, 1½ in. thick
1 teaspoon salt
¼ teaspoon pepper
¼ cup flour
2 tablespoons fat

1 clove garlic, minced
2 large onions, sliced
1 tablespoon Worcestershire sauce
2 8-oz. cans tomato sauce
1 dash red hot sauce

Trim fat edges from meat. Combine salt, pepper, flour. Divide in half and pound half of mixture into each side of steak. Heat fat in heavy frypan and brown meat quickly on both sides. Add remaining ingredients, cover, reduce to simmer and cook about 2 hours or until meat is tender. If desired, thicken sauce before serving with meat. Serves 6.

GOLDEN ONION GRAVY FOR STEAK

4 cups sliced onions
2 tablespoons fat
2 tablespoons flour
2 cups meat stock

1 tablespoon Worcestershire sauce
salt
freshly ground pepper

Heat fat in heavy frypan and cook onions until light golden brown. Gradually stir in flour, stirring until smooth. Add remaining ingredients; reduce heat very low and cook until thick, stirring constantly. Cover and simmer 10 minutes. Serves 6.

•

BARBECUED SHORT RIBS

Using 3 pounds beef short ribs, cut meat from bones into serving pieces. Marinate overnight in Southern Barbecue Sauce Supreme or your favorite sauce. Grill over hot charcoal, brushing often with barbecue sauce and turning to brown.

SPANISH BEEFBURGERS

½ cup finely chopped onions
¼ cup chopped celery
¼ cup chopped green pepper
3 tablespoons melted butter
1 can condensed tomato soup
2 tablespoons Worcestershire sauce

2 tablespoons vinegar
1 tablespoon prepared mustard
1 pound ground beef, shaped into
    patties
bacon grease

Cook onions, celery and green pepper in butter until onions are transparent. Add all remaining ingredients except beef; mix well and simmer 10 minutes; stirring several times. In frypan, brown beef patties in bacon grease and cook until done. Place each patty on toasted roll, pour hot Spanish sauce over and serve hot. Serves 4 or 5.

OLD FASHIONED FRIED TRIPE

(As early Floridians cooked this, it melted in the mouth. The secret was overnight marinating in cold water and several table-spoons of vinegar—the early American tenderizer.)

2 pounds tripe
4 tablespoons vinegar
2 peppercorns
salt, pepper

1 beaten egg
2 teaspoons water
seasoned flour
lemon wedges

Soak tripe overnight in water and 3 tablespoons vinegar. Pour off water; place meat in water to cover and add 1 tablespoon vinegar and peppercorns. Simmer until tender, which may take up to 4 hours. Again, leave tripe in this liquid until ready to fry. Cut into serving size pieces. Dip into beaten egg mixed with water then into seasoned flour. Saute in hot fat until crisp and golden brown. Serve with lemon wedges.

GREEN CABBAGE ROLLS

1½ lb. ground round beef
1 medium onion, chopped
1 teaspoon salt
¼ teaspoon pepper
1 egg

1 cup cooked rice
½ can water
1 can tomato soup
1 head green cabbage

Mix first 6 ingredients together; set aside. Blend ½ soup can of water with soup; reserve. Place cabbage head in one inch of boiling water, stem end down. As leaves become soft, remove and set aside. On each leaf, place ½ cup of meat mixture; roll and fold leaf ends under. Place in baking dish and cover with soup mixture. Cover and bake one hour at 375 deg. Makes 8 servings.

SEMINOLE INDIANS

The pride of the Seminole people, shown in this woman's face, led them to fight for their right to Florida lands.

Think of the Everglades and you think of Seminole Indians, yet they are not natives of Florida! When the Spanish first set foot in Florida they found some 10,000 Indians. Among them were the Calusas, fishermen and mariners in southwest Florida who violently opposed the white man's advance, and the Apalachee of the northwest, semi-civilized and powerful with a strong league of united chiefs.

After the English-Spanish struggle caused by the settling of Georgia and the Carolinas resulted in an English victory and James E. Oglethorpe founded Savannah in 1733, he swept south into Florida. A disastrous war had recently wiped out most of Florida's native Indians, and allies from the Lower Creek tribes came with Oglethorpe to help him fight. They liked the land and decided to stay.

Other Lower Creeks settled in the Apalachee region or moved into other north Florida areas. About 1775, their name became Seminole meaning runaway. By 1835, they were firmly settled

and determined not to move. The seven towns they had in 1799
rapidly increased to 20 or more.

Hostilities with the U.S. began while the Spanish were still
in control, especially during the War of 1812 and again in 1817-18,
now called the first Seminole War. Gen. Andrew Jackson quelled
the latter with 3,000 men—one reason for Spain ceding the territory to the U.S. in 1819.

By the St. Moultrie treaty in 1823, the Seminole ceded most
of their lands except a central reservation. But pressure continued
for their complete removal, so another treaty was negotiated at
Payne's Landing in 1832, which compelled them to move west of
the Mississippi within three years.

Most of the tribe, under Osceola's leadership, repudiated this
last treaty, and so began the second war in 1835. It ended in
August, 1842, and most of the tribe was moved west. But the
cost was great—1,466 American lives and $20,000,000.

Some 300 Seminoles escaped into the watery wilderness of
the Everglades and by 1960, this number had grown to slightly
over 1,000. Far from being resented, the Indians are now a valu-
able asset in a tourist-oriented state.

Until 1960, most lived in "chickees"—a shelter without walls
made with four poles, wooden floor and palm-thatched roof. Until
millions of new residents cut severely into the hunting and fishing
which was the food source for the tribe, the Indians lived a peace-
able life among the animals and birds of the Everglades. They
had three reservations, in Glades County, Broward County and
Hendry County. However, in recent years they have found it
necessary to organize under a Federal charter, become cattle
ranchers and operators of a successful arts and crafts center and
the Okalee Indian Village (open to tourists) on Dania plantation.

The Cow Creek Seminoles have learned to live and cooperate
with the white man, although they have never accepted him. But
the Mikasuki, many of whom live along Tamiami Trail and operate
restaurants and tourist attractions, are more antagonistic and
less prosperous.

The Seminoles have always been a proud race, self-reliant,
tenacious of their opinions, true to the traditions of their race,
with life based on matrilineal lineage. So a camp is usually com-
posed of a woman, her daughters, and their children, and the
husbands and unmarried brothers of these. When a man marries,
he goes to his wife's camp, builds her a house and moves in.

Each household must contain the all-important sewing machine used to make the rainbow-colored, long-skirted costumes of the women and the shirts of the men. Youngsters are now wearing modern dress, but the traditional costumes are still worn by elders of the tribe.

In their new homes, the Indians have electric ranges, but cooking is still done the old, primitive way deep in the reservations. The camp fire is unique. Several logs are arranged like spokes of a wheel, with the fire at the hub. Ends of the long logs extend into the fire and are continually pushed over the flame as it burns the wood.

Over this fire hangs a black iron pot filled with Soffkee, the standby food. This is a stew of meat, usually venison with meal, grits and vegetables added. A wooden spoon is used and each one dips out a spoonful of stew when he feels hungry, any time of the day.

Their fruits are guavas, sour oranges and limes, bananas, wild berries and plums. In cleared land on the hummock, they grow corn, pumpkins, melons, sweet potatoes and sugar cane. Tender buds of the palmetto (called hearts of palm by the white man) are eaten year-round, raw or cooked.

When hunting is good, the men bag deer, quail, wild turkey, opossum, rabbit, squirrel; and from Florida waters they take fish, turtles and oysters. When hunting is poor, they eat the chickens and pigs raised at home.

Koonti is the staff of life, the equivalent of our wheat bread. This is a wild cassava root that grows only in extreme south Florida and is called "God's gift to the Seminole." Very nutritious, it tastes something like arrowroot.

The Seminoles mash this root to pulp in mortars cut into cypress logs called koonti logs. The starch is then separated from the pulp with a straining cloth, yielding a yellowish-white flour used to bake their bright orange bread. At one time, koonti starch was used in food and for laundry and koonti-making was quite an industry in south Florida.

Several chiefs of the tribe have served as Baptist ministers, and many of the Indians have become Christians. Today, their aim is to enjoy modern living, give their children good educations, but never to surrender their revered Indian traditions.

TIP: Rubbing a wild duck with lemon will help kill the gamey taste.

SKILLET ORANGE DUCK

1/3 cup all purpose flour	1½ cups water
1½ teaspoons salt	1/3 cup cooking sherry
¼ teaspoon pepper	1/3 cup orange juice
3 ducks, quartered	2 tablespoons orange marmalade
1/3 cup butter	1 tablespoon grated orange rind

In bag, combine flour, salt, pepper, and shake duck in bag. Over medium heat in heavy iron skillet, brown duck in butter. Combine all remaining ingredients and pour over duck. Cover; simmer 1½ hours or until tender. Serves 6.

VENISON SOUP

1 3-lb. venison roast	4 onions, cubed
4 cups cold water	1 clove garlic, chopped fine
1 tablespoon salt	1 bay leaf
1½ quarts water	1 tablespoon parsley
1 bunch celery hearts, sliced	flour
2 cups tomatoes	salt, pepper
3 medium potatoes, cubed	

Soak roast in cold salt water overnight. Discard water and put meat in 1½ quarts water. Simmer for 2½ hours; remove and cool meat. Place in refrigerator overnight. Next day, skim off fat, simmer 2 hours; 20 minutes before meat is done, add celery, tomatoes, potatoes, onions, garlic, bay leaf. Add parsley. Season to taste with salt and pepper. If necessary, thicken with a little flour. Serves 6 to 8.

OYSTER CORN BREAD STUFFING FOR WILD TURKEY

6 tablespoons butter	1 pint oysters with liquid
¼ cup minced onion	¾ teaspoon salt
4 cups crumbled cornbread	¼ teaspoon paprika
2 lightly beaten eggs	2 tablespoons minced parsley

Melt butter and saute onion until golden brown. Stir in all remaining ingredients. Toss lightly to mix. Cool before stuffing bird.

FRIED GREEN TOMATOES

Use three mature, firm green tomatoes. Wash, dry and cut in thick slices. Sprinkle with salt, let stand 5 minutes then drain. Sprinkle with freshly ground black pepper. Dredge in corn meal and fry in hot fat until lightly browned. Serve hot. Makes 4 servings.

BOILED HARDSHELL CRABS

Using 12 live hardshell crabs, plunge into boiling salted water in heavy large pot, cover and boil 15 to 20 minutes, or until red. Serve on heated platter with cracking tools and individual dishes of melted butter for each person. Crack shells and pick out the meat on underside of the shell and from the claws, also the tamale or green liver.

CORN HOECAKE

Combine 2 cups white cornmeal with 1 teaspoon salt. Add enough boiling water (it must be boiling hot) to make a medium batter. Let stand for 1 hour. Heat bacon grease in a heavy frypan and place a heaping tablespoon full of batter in hot pan. Press down lightly with spatula to make cakes ½-inch thick. When one side is golden brown, turn and brown the other. Serve very hot. Specially good with turnip greens.

SWAMP CABBAGE
(Heart of the Florida cabbage or palmetto palm)

Chop the heart out of a cabbage palm tree. Trim off the tough boots on the outside until you reach the center of the palm heart. Each frond makes a layer or boot which has to be removed individually by splitting full length. Then lower part of palm heart is reached, and the bud is cut into ½-inch chunks. Boil rapidly about 30 minutes in plenty of salted water in open pot. Add 1 tablespoon bacon drippings for flavor. Stir frequently to prevent sticking.

ROASTING EARS

Using 4 ears unhusked fresh sweet corn, remove outer husks and tassels. Leave inner husks on corn. In deep pot, submerge corn in 4 quarts of water with 6 tablespoons salt. Weight corn to hold it under water and soak 1 hour. Remove corn from water, place 1 teaspoon butter inside the ear on the kernels, wrap in aluminum foil and roast in 450 deg. oven about 25 minutes or until done. Serve hot with dish of melted butter, plenty of salt and pepper. Serves 4. (Note: Corn may also be roasted amid hot coals in barbecue pit—have coals well burned down with no flames—and cook about 10 minutes.)

BLACK-EYED PEAS WITH DUMPLINGS

1 cup dried black-eyed peas	DUMPLINGS:
3 cups water	2 cups flour
1 teaspoon salt	4 teaspoons baking powder
2 oz. boiling bacon or 1 tablespoon	1 teaspoon salt
cooking oil	about 1 cup milk

Wash peas, cover with 3 cups water and soak overnight. Add salt and meat or oil to peas; bring to boil then reduce to simmer and cook covered until beans are tender; 15 minutes before end of cooking time, remove cover. Sift dry ingredients together, then add enough milk to make dough. If necessary, add more water to have about one cup liquid in pot. With fork and spoon, drop walnut-sized bits into peas, cover pot tightly; steam 15 minutes.

SEMINOLE PUMPKIN BREAD

The Seminoles use cooked, mashed pumpkin mixed with self-rising flour and water to make a soft dough. They knead it in a ball until it is elastic then continue turning and folding until it is about ¼-inch thick. Small cakes are placed in a heavy iron skillet filled with smoking grease and fried until golden brown on each side. This makes a puffy, crisp bread. Here is a modern version of the traditional Indian bread, made with pumpkin but baked in the oven.

Using a unique 4-log fire, a Seminole woman prepares pumpkin bread.

BAKED PUMPKIN BREAD

1½ cups sifted flour	1 cup mashed pumpkin
1¼ teaspoons soda	1 cup sugar
1 teaspoon salt	½ cup buttermilk
1 teaspoon ground cinnamon	1 egg, slightly beaten
½ teaspoon ground nutmeg	2 tablespoons soft butter

Sift together twice flour, soda, salt and spices. In large bowl, mix well pumpkin, sugar, buttermilk and slightly beaten egg. Stir in dry ingredients and butter. Beat at medium speed until blended. Turn into loaf pan and bake at 350 deg. for 1 hour.

FRIED FROGS LEGS

Soak frogs' legs in equal amounts of salt water and milk for 1 hour. Drain; pat dry. Shake in bag of seasoned flour. Saute in hot oil or butter until tender and brown. Serve with lemon or lime wedges.

BAKED RABBIT

Skin and dress rabbit and cut into serving pieces. Shake in a bag of flour seasoned with salt and pepper. Fry in butter or bacon drippings until golden brown. Place in baking dish; cover with milk. Bake in 350 deg. oven about 1 hour or until tender. Mix a little flour with water and use to thicken milk for gravy. Pour over rabbit; serve hot.

After Tallahassee was named territorial government seat, lawmakers met in this three-story Capitol building.

From Tallahassee to Gainesville, time has not touched the fairy tale beauty of the gently rolling red clay hills, azure lakes and great live oaks trailing Spanish moss. The Suwannee River meanders lazily across the state between banks of lush green, shadowed by the spreading arms of ancient trees.

To the north and west, almost in the center of the panhandle, lies Tallahassee, a Creek Indian word meaning "Old Town." The north Florida area was first explored by Panfilo de Narvaez who landed at Tampa Bay in 1528. So fierce was the Indian opposition to his march that only four men returned to tell of the trip.

A year later, he was followed by Hernando de Soto who took his men north into Georgia, fighting Indians all the way past an Indian village near the modern city of Ocala, and into Tallahassee.

The city's first item of recorded history is dated 1539, when de Soto held a powwow with the controlling Apalachee tribes, but this must have been a center for Indian activity long before that. De Soto wintered near Tallahassee with a 600-man party, and it is believed that this marked the first observance of Christmas in the New World.

In the 17th century, Spanish missions were strung out on the Suwannee in north Florida from St. Augustine to the Gulf. One of these was the Spanish Mission of San Luis, established in 1633 near Tallahassee.

The Old World first learned of the beauty of the Suwannee River country with its springs and underground caverns when, just after the Revolutionary War in 1791, famous travel writer and botanist William Bartram published a book describing his Florida travels.

Titled *The Travels of William Bartram* and still in print, the book recreated the beauty of the region so well that it is believed by some scholars to have inspired many lines in Coleridge's poem, "Kubla Khan".

In 1812, Georgia settlers established a Republic of Florida. They were tormented by repeated Indian raids from tribes to the south until General Andrew Jackson swept down into Florida in 1814 to do battle. His victories weakened the hold of Spain on Florida cities, forcing the Spanish to sell Florida to the United States for $5 million in 1819.

It was on March 4, 1824 that Tallahassee came into its own, when it was named the capital of the Territory of Florida.

During its first half century, the city saw rowdy backwoodsmen mingling on the streets with wealthy planters from Georgia, North Carolina and Virginia.

Social life was lively and festive, led by such celebrities as Prince Achille Murat, nephew of Napoleon Bonaparte. The Prince bought a large plantation near Tallahassee and married Catherine Willis, great-grandniece of George Washington, in Tallahassee. He recorded details of the elaborate dinner parties in his journal, writing, "No news in town except a wine party, or rather eating, drinking, card playing and segar smoking."

The burial place of the Prince and his lady is in the Episcopal Cemetery, one of the town sights.

The longest and costliest of America's Indian wars raged from 1833 to 1842, finally forcing the Seminoles to abandon their beloved hill country and flee south for safety into the Everglades.

The inflow of settlers increased and by 1845, there were many great plantations in north Florida raising cotton and sugar cane, producing cattle and hogs. The pretentious Maryland and Virginia late-Georgian Colonial mansions built then still stand, giving the area a genuine aura of the Old South.

Less elaborate but equally well proportioned are at least a dozen more mansions built in the 1830's in the ante-bellum towns of Madison, Monticello, Quincy and Marianna.

A gracious pattern of life developed on the plantations of people from the Carolinas, Virginia, Georgia and Alabama, and it has continued to this day. Under twinkling chandeliers, the cream of Florida's political and social set still gathers to feast on lavish spreads of good food, mostly in the Southern tradition.

This has been retained because south Florida's boom skipped past this part of the state, so the old-time beauty and charm remains largely intact. What began as a 15-home settlement was a city with 48,174 residents by 1960. But Tallahassee has not succumbed to the cosmopolitanism of a tourist state.

Still there are the stately, white-columned homes furnished with rare antiques. Also magnificent gardens aflame with camellia, japonica and azalea each spring; and Civil War trenches and breastworks in the town park; and the State Capitol and Governor's mansion.

Since 1857, Tallahassee has been the home of the Florida State University; since 1887, of the Florida Agricultural and Mechanical University.

In this placid land of magnolias and oleanders, the mint julep is popular and Southern food is still king. From nearby farmlands come garden vegetables, sweet potatoes, watermelons, pecans, corn, peanuts, Irish potatoes, sugar cane.

Game birds, home-grown beef, hogs and chickens are plentiful. Fried chicken, cornbread and biscuits, fruit puddings and pies, rich milk and cream desserts—these are among the homemade dishes still served with warm hospitality in north Florida homes.

GREEN BEAN SALAD

3 cups cooked green beans, drained
2 cups cooked English peas, drained
¼ cup stuffed olives, sliced
¼ cup almonds, sliced
2 cups celery cut in ½-inch strips

1 cup green onions, sliced
2 cups raw carrots in ½-inch strips
2 slices bacon, cooked, drained and crumbled

Combine ingredients except bacon and marinate overnight in French dressing. Drain before serving. Crumble bacon over top just before serving.

CHICKEN MOUSSE

2 envelopes gelatin
¼ cup cold water
½ cup boiling chicken stock
1 cup cool stock
1 teaspoon Worcestershire sauce
salt and pepper to taste

2 cups diced white chicken meat
1 cup diced celery
½ cup mayonnaise
½ cup cup heavy cream, whipped
1/3 cup grated almonds
2 teaspoons chopped parsley

Soften gelatin in cold water. Stir into hot stock until dissolved then combine with cool stock, Worcestershire sauce, salt and pepper. Refrigerate until consistency is like honey. Add all remaining ingredients. Turn into oiled mold. Chill till set then unmold and garnish with parsley. Serves 6. If desired, serve with chilled watermelon pickles.

WILLIE'S CHICKEN DRESSING

(Guests frequently skip the chicken to eat this superb dressing.)

3 cups crumbled cornbread
3 cups crumbled biscuits
1 teaspoon salt
1 teaspoon poultry seasoning

2 medium onions, chopped fine
3 celery stalks, chopped fine
1 cup pecans, chopped fine

Night before, boil chicken giblets in one quart of salted water to get stock. Mix together all ingredients; add enough stock to moisten. Pack into square, greased baking pan and bake in 350 deg. oven until brown, 25-30 minutes. (May also be used to stuff the bird instead of being baked separately.)

CHICKEN GIBLET GRAVY

chicken giblets and neck
1 teaspoon salt
4 peppercorns
1 onion, stuck with 4 cloves

1 carrot, scraped
3 tablespoons flour
1 hard-cooked egg, chopped

Put giblets in one quart of water with salt, peppercorns, onion, carrot; bring to boil then reduce heat to simmer. Cook until tender. Chop giblets and bits of neck meat. Strain in broth. Take chicken from roasting pan and pour out drippings. For 2 cups gravy, return 3 tablespoons drippings to pan. Over low heat, blend in 3 tablespoons flour, stirring constantly. Use 2 cups giblet broth, pour 1 cup into roast pan, stirring until brown bits are loose. Then add remaining 1 cup, stir until very smooth and hot. Stir in chopped giblets and chopped, hard-cooked egg. Correct seasoning.

FLORIDA FRENCH DRESSING

1/3 cup orange juice
1 cup salad oil
¼ cup vinegar
½ teaspoon Worcestershire sauce
½ teaspoon paprika

½ clove garlic
2 tablespoons lemon juice
1/3 cup confectioners sugar
½ teaspoon salt
¼ teaspoon dry mustard

Mix altogether and shake in jar until blended. Makes 1½ cups.

SOUTHERN MASHED POTATO SALAD

8 to 10 medium potatoes
1½ teaspoon salt
¼ teaspoon pepper
¼ cup cider vinegar
1¼ cups mayonnaise

6 hard-cooked eggs, chopped
1 small jar pimientos, chopped
½ cup chopped green onion tops
¾ cup chopped green pepper
1 cup chopped celery

Boil potatoes in salted water, covered, until tender. Drain well. In pot, mash until smooth. Stir in thoroughly salt, pepper, vinegar and mayonnaise. Add eggs and all other ingredients; toss gently. Pack into ring mold, turn out and serve while warm. Or chill if desired. Serves 10.

CRISP GREEN TOMATO PICKLES

4 quarts thinly sliced green tomatoes
1 quart thinly sliced white onions
1/3 cup salt
3 cups white vinegar
1 teaspoon whole allspice
2 teaspoons whole black pepper

1 tablespoon celery seed
2 tablespoons white mustard seed
1 lemon, thinly sliced
2 drops red hot sauce
3 cups packed brown sugar

Sprinkle 1/3 cup salt on tomatoes and onion; leave overnight, covered. Drain. Place all remaining ingredients in pot; bring to boil and add tomatoes and onion. Bring to boil then reduce to simmer and cook about 10 minutes, stirring several times. Pour into hot sterilized jars and seal. Makes 5 pints.

HONEY FRUIT SALAD DRESSING

1 cup cream, whipped
3 tablespoons honey

1 tablespoon lime or lemon juice
1/8 teaspoon mace

Beat cream just until stiff then beat in remaining ingredients. Use as dessert sauce over fresh or canned peaches, pineapple, pears, or other fruit.

SUNSHINE CHICKEN SALAD

1½ cups cooked diced chicken
¾ cup diced celery
½ cup white grapes, halved
½ cup Creamy Fruit Dressing

salad greens
½ avocado, sliced
¼ cup chopped pecans
6 canned spiced crabapples

Add Creamy Fruit Dressing to chicken, celery and grapes. Place greens on plates with salad in center. Sprinkle with chopped pecans; garnish with sliced avocado and crabapples. Serves 6.

Through the window drifts the rich aroma of Yam Praline Pie.

CREAMY FRUIT DRESSING

2 teaspoons salt
1 teaspoon sugar
½ teaspoon paprika

½ cup lemon juice
1½ cups salad oil
1-1/3 cups light cream

In jar, shake together all ingredients except cream. Gradually add the cream, beating with rotary beater until thick. Makes 3-1/3 cups; may be cut in half for about 1¾ cups.

YAM PRALINE PIE

2 eggs
½ cup granulated sugar
½ cup packed light brown sugar
1 teaspoon cinnamon
½ teaspoon nutmeg
½ teaspoon ginger

¼ teaspoon salt
2 cups mashed cooked fresh yams
¾ cup milk
1 cup light cream
1 unbaked 9-inch pastry shell
1/3 cup chopped pecans

Beat eggs in mixing bowl; beat in granulated and brown sugars, spices and salt. Blend in yams. Gradually stir in milk and cream. Pour into unbaked pastry shell. Bake in 400 deg. oven 10 minutes. Reduce heat to 350 deg. and bake 20 minutes. Sprinkle Praline Topping over surface of pie. Continue baking 25 minutes until knife inserted near center comes out clean. Cool completely before serving. (To make Praline Topping, mix together 1/3 cup chopped pecans, ½ cup packed brown sugar and 3 tablespoons soft butter.)

CREOLE SWEET POTATO PECAN PIE

9-inch unbaked pie shell
1/3 cup granulated white sugar
1/3 cup light brown sugar
¼ teaspoon salt
¾ teaspoon ground ginger
¾ teaspoon ground cinnamon
½ teaspoon ground nutmeg
1/16 teaspoon ground cloves

1 cup mashed sweet potatoes
2 well beaten eggs
¾ cup hot milk
½ cup light brown sugar
¼ cup (½ stick) butter or margarine, softened
¾ cup pecans, chopped medium fine

Line 9-inch pie plate with unbaked pastry; set aside. Combine white and brown sugars, salt and spices in mixing bowl. Blend in mashed sweet potatoes. Beat in eggs. Stir in hot milk. Pour into unbaked pie shell. Bake 25 minutes in preheated 375 deg. oven. Meanwhile, blend ½ cup brown sugar with butter or margarine and pecans. Sprinkle over partially baked pie. Continue baking 30 minutes or until filling is firm in center. Serve cold with whipped cream.

MOCK OYSTERS

1 cup corn cut from cob (or frozen)
1 tablespoon butter, melted
2 egg yolks, separated
½ teaspoon salt
⅛ teaspoon ground black pepper

dash cayenne
¼ teaspoon ground thyme
½ cup sifted all-purpose flour
celery salt

Combine corn, butter, egg yolks, seasoning and flour. Beat egg whites until they stand in soft, stiff peaks and fold into mixture. Drop from teaspoon into deep fat preheated to 350 deg. Fry until golden. Drain on paper towels. Sprinkle lightly with celery salt. Serve as appetizers. Makes 60.

GLORIFIED SUMMER SQUASH

2 cups cooked yellow squash
¾ cup bread crumbs
3 tablespoons butter
½ cup milk
2 tablespoons chopped onion
2 tablespoons chopped green pepper
1 tablespoons chopped pimiento

2 tablespoons tomato catsup
salt, pepper to taste
¾ cup grated Cheddar cheese
2 beaten eggs
1 cup buttered bread crumbs
paprika

Boil squash in salted water until tender. Mash fine; add all other ingredients. Pour into buttered baking dish. Top with buttered bread crumbs; sprinkle with paprika. Bake in 350 deg. oven until firm 25 to 30 minutes. Serves 4-6.

OLD SOUTH TOMATO SALAD

3 medium tomatoes, sliced
1 onion cut into rings
salad greens
1/3 cup French salad dressing
¾ teaspoon celery seed

¼ cup pickle relish
6 slices crisp cooked bacon, crumbled
2 hard-cooked eggs, quartered
monosodium glutamate

On crisp greens, place tomatoes and onion rings. Blend French dressing with celery seed and pickle relish; pour over tomatoes and onions. Sprinkle with monosodium glutamate; scatter bacon on top and garnish with eggs. Serves 6

SOUTHERN CORN PUDDING

3 eggs
2 cups cream style canned corn
2 tablespoons melted butter
2 cups scalded milk
2 teaspoons salt, dash of pepper

2 tablespoons flour
1 tablespoon sugar
cracker crumbs
butter

Beat eggs well. Combine with all ingredients. Pour into buttered casserole. Sprinkle with crumbs; dot with butter. Place in pan of warm water. Bake in 325 deg. oven, uncovered, 1 hour 15 minutes. Makes 6 servings.

DEVILED FRESH CARROTS

12 young tender carrots
½ cup butter or margarine
2 tablespoons light brown sugar
¾ teaspoon salt

1 teaspoon powdered mustard
⅛ teaspoon ground black pepper
dash cayenne pepper

Wash carrots, peel and cut each in half lengthwise. Saute in butter 5 minutes. Add salt and spices. Cover and cook 10 minutes or until carrots are tender. Serve hot. Serves 6.

BUTTERMILK BISCUITS

2 cups flour
2 teaspoons baking powder
¼ teaspoon soda

1 teaspoon salt
1 cup buttermilk (about)
2 tablespoons lard or ham fat

Measure 2 heaping tablespoons of flour and use to flour surface. Put remaining flour in bowl, make a hole in center of flour and put into this the baking powder, baking soda and salt. Add shortening; pour in buttermilk. With finger tips, gradually mix, using enough milk to make a soft dough. Turn onto floured surface and pat gently to ½ inch thickness. Cut out with biscuit cutter and place in greased pan. Bake at 400 deg. until brown on bottom (about 15 minutes) then place under broiler for a minute or two, if necessary to brown tops. Makes about 20 biscuits.

PECAN WAFFLES

2 cups sifted all-purpose flour
1 teaspoon baking soda
1 tablespoon sugar
½ teaspoon salt
2 eggs, separated

¼ cup vinegar
1¾ cups sweet milk
1/3 cup melted shortening
¾ cup chopped pecans

Sift together flour, baking soda, sugar and salt. Beat together egg yolks, vinegar, milk then mix with dry ingredients. Stir in melted shortening and pecans, stirring until smooth. Use mixer to beat egg whites till stiff but not dry; fold into batter. Pour on heated waffle iron; bake until steaming stops. Serve with warm syrup and butter.

HONEY PECAN BANANA BREAD

1¼ cups shortening
2 cups sugar
4 eggs
1 cup honey
2½ cups mashed ripe bananas

5 cups sifted all-purpose flour
2½ teaspoons baking powder
2½ teaspoons baking soda
1 teaspoon salt
2 cups chopped pecans

Cream shortening and sugar. Add eggs one at a time while creaming. Add honey and bananas; mix thoroughly. Sift flour, baking powder, soda and salt together. Add to liquid ingredients, mixing well. Fold in chopped pecans. Pour in three 4x8x2½ inch loaf pans, lightly greased on bottom and sides, slightly more than ¾ full. Bake in 350 deg. oven 45 to 55 minutes or until tester comes out clean. Makes 3 loaves.

HONEY PECAN PIE

single 9-inch pie crust
3 eggs
1/3 cup granulated sugar
1/3 cup light brown sugar
¼ teaspoon salt

¼ cup melted butter
½ cup honey
½ cup white corn syrup
1 teaspoon vanilla
1 cup pecan halves

Beat eggs. Mix in all other ingredients except pecan halves; pour into pastry-lined 9-inch pie pan. Arrange pecan halves on filling in desired pattern. Bake 40 to 50 minutes at 375 deg. until set and pastry is golden. Cool. Serve cold or slightly warm.

FLORIDA PANHANDLE

Steep steps climb the crumbling brick wall of Fort San Carlos, built in Fernandina after 1784.

History was made in Pensacola, the second oldest city in the United States. In four centuries, the people have lived under 17 changes of government, and five flags—Spanish, French, British, Confederate, and American.

The first colony was founded when Tristan de Luna landed in Pensacola Bay with 1500 persons in 1559, but a hurricane hit the fleet and the venture ended in just two years. Today, a cross in the sand is a reminder of the event.

After establishing St. Augustine, the Spanish returned to Pensacola in 1698 to build a fort. The French moved down the Mississippi and took the fort in 1719 but lost it again to the Spanish, and so it went.

After Great Britain ceded Florida to Spain in 1783, there were frequent Indian raids and Andrew Jackson waged successful attacks in Florida, then set up a military government in 1818. In 1821, he became provisional governor when Spain gave Florida up to the U. S., and Pensacola was his headquarters.

Important because it is the state's largest natural deep-water harbor, Pensacola had a U.S. Navy Yard built in 1825 and has remained an important military bastion ever since.

Fort Pickens on Santa Rosa Island was a key Union stronghold during the War Between the States, when Union forces held the fort and imprisoned Geronimo and his Apaches.

Inside famous Pensacola Naval Air Station, where naval aviation was born, are Forts San Carlos, Barrancas and Redoubt.

The Confederates were ordered to abandon the city in February, 1862; supplies and troops were moved out. Most citizens left, burning what they could not carry, and by May, Federal troops took over. There was a long listless period followed by the Reconstruction, then the timber and naval stores in the area began moving out on new railroads.

The waterfront was improved during the busy 1870's, berthing ships from Italy and France, from England and Sweden. A disastrous fire swept the town in 1880, but by 1900, Pensacola was the second largest city in Florida, with 18,000 residents.

The Government built its first training base for naval aviators there in 1914. This is one of the events recorded in the history of Naval aviation from its beginnings to the space age, which is shown in the Naval Air Museum at the Naval Air Station.

This quiet city is thriving, but life continues at a pleasant, leisurely pace. Summers, this westernmost section of Florida is filled with Southern tourists flocking to the magnificent beaches of Santa Rosa Island, part of a great state park which offers swimming, fishing boating. The beaches are famous for their long stretches of pure white sand.

Hunting for quail, turkey and deer is done in Apalachicola National Forest, which spreads over 600,000 acres and is the largest of the state's three national forests. And for fishing buffs, there is fun to be had angling for fine specimens of red snapper, tarpon, channel bass, sea trout, mackerel, amberjack, grouper, and more, from old Pensacola Bay Bridge—"the world's longest fishing pier."

Pensacola itself is more Spanish than American and the wrought iron decorating the houses is a tipoff that, historically and architecturally, the town is more closely related to New Orleans and Mobile than to Florida cities. Old balconies, graceful gables and wrought-iron balustrades contribute to the romantic, Old World atmosphere along oak-shaded streets.

Pensacola has a proud group of "Creoles" with a combined Negro-Spanish heritage, as well as a prosperous Negro population. Traditional cooking of the Old South blends with all the varied nationalities to create a unique cuisine.

It's an old Pensacola custom to have a Hospitality Table near the front door of each home at Christmas time, laden with fruit and homemade goodies.

Southern foods take on added Spanish and Creole spiciness in the steaming seafood chowders, crusty brown barbecued chicken and fish, Gaspachee (better known as Gazpacho) salad, homemade mincement, baked grits, Hoppin' John, and much more.

In magnolia-shaded Pensacola, and in other Florida cities along the Gulf Coast—Fort Walton Beach, Panama City, Apalachicola—the unique handling of fresh seafood is superb, not to be missed!

PANHANDLE SPECIALTIES

OYSTERS ROCKEFELLER

1/ cup grated onion	⅛ teaspoon pepper
¼ cup finely chopped parsley	few drops Tabasco
3 tablespoons finely chopped celery	½ cup butter
1 teaspoon lemon juice	3 dozen oysters on the half shell
¼ teaspoon salt	buttered crumbs

Cream butter then add onion, parsley, celery, lemon juice and seasonings. Place oysters on half shell in shallow baking pan. Top each with a spoonful of the onion and butter mixture. Sprinkle with buttered crumbs and bake in 375 deg. oven about 30 minutes, until crumbs are brown. Serves 6.

DEVILED CRABS

1 pound crabmeat	1 tablespoon vinegar
1 cup cracker crumbs	1 tablespoon Worcestershire sauce
3 eggs, lightly beaten	½ teaspoon salt
½ cup finely minced celery	½ teaspoon black pepper
½ cup minced green pepper	few drops Tabasco
2 tablespoons lemon juice	1 cup melted butter

Beat eggs lightly. Mix all ingredients lightly. Stuff into 8 crab shells. Bake at 375 deg. for about 12 minutes, until piping hot. Serves 8.

SHE-CRAB SOUP

(She-crabs make a more tasty soup because the eggs add richness.)

1 medium onion, chopped fine	1 cup cooked small lima beans
2 tablespoons butter	salt, pepper to taste
2 cups she-crab with eggs	1 teaspoon Worcestershire sauce
1 tablespoon flour	⅛ teaspoon mace
4 cups milk	4 tablespoons dry sherry
1 cup cooked grated corn	½ cup heavy cream, whipped

Melt butter in top of double boiler and blend with flour until smooth. Add milk gradually, stirring constantly. Add crabmeat with eggs, stir slowly and let

From Florida waters, a platter of succulent Oysters Rockerfeller.

boil about 10 minutes. Stir in corn, lima beans, seasonings. Simmer 10 minutes. To serve, place 1 tablespoon of warmed sherry in each soup bowl. Add soup; top with whipped cream. If desired, sprinkle with paprika. (Note: If she-crabs cannot be had, crumble yolk of hard-cooked egg in bottom of soup bowls.) Serves 6.

SHRIMP CREOLE

½ pound salt pork
2 medium onions, chopped
1 medium green pepper, chopped
2 celery stalks, chopped
2 cans tomatoes

1 can tomato soup
1 can tomato paste
salt, pepper, Worcestershire to taste
3 pounds shrimp
2 cups rice

Dice salt pork and fry until crisp and brown in heavy skillet. Remove bacon from pan, leaving all melted fat in skillet. Add chopped onions, pepper, and celery to fat; simmer until soft. Add tomatoes, soup, tomato paste. Season to taste with salt, pepper, Worcestershire. Cook on low heat until thick, about 2 hours, stirring occasionally.

While sauce is cooking, prepare shrimp. Rinse well under cool, running water. Cook in large pot containing 3 or more quarts of boiling, salted water 10 to 12 minutes, just until shells turn pink. Remove from heat, cool in cooking water about 20 minutes, drain. When cool, remove shells and de-vein. Add shrimp to cooked sauce, saving 6-8 large shrimp to garnish top. Cook 2 cups rice; cover with Shrimp Creole and garnish. Serves 8.

PICKLED SHRIMP

1 cup salad oil
1 cup white vinegar
juice of ½ lemon
1 teaspoon dill seed
1 teaspoon peppercorns

1 stick cinnamon
1 teaspoon cloves
1 teaspoon salt
1 onion, sliced
2 lbs. cleaned, boiled shrimp

Cook together for 10 minutes first 8 ingredients. Cool. Slice onion and place in bowl with cold shrimp. Pour pickling mixture over shrimp; refrigerate overnight. (Keeps well up to a week.) Drain; serve as appetizer, or on salad plate.

GASPACHEE (PENSACOLA SALAD)

2 hardtack or pilot bread
2 chopped cucumbers
2 chopped large ripe tomatoes
1 chopped green pepper

1 medium onion, chopped
4 chopped stalks of celery
about ¾ cup mayonnaise
salt, pepper to taste

Soak hardtack in water at least one hour. Squeeze dry of all water; add vegetable ingredients, mayonnaise, salt and pepper. (Be sure the vegetables are very finely chopped and well chilled, for best flavor.)

BAKED GRITS

1 cup milk
2 tablespoons butter
2 cups cooked grits

2 eggs beaten until frothy
½ teaspoon salt
dash of pepper

Heat milk and butter. Add and mix until smooth the grits, eggs, salt and pepper. Pour into buttered casserole and bake at 325 degrees until firm and golden brown, about 35 minutes. Serves 4-6.

SOUTHERN SPOON BREAD

(Every Florida pioneer has a favorite recipe.)

4 cups milk
1 cup white corn meal
2 tablespoons butter
1½ teaspoons salt

1 teaspoon double-acting baking
powder
4 well-beaten eggs

Over hot water in double boiler, scald milk; gradually add corn meal and continue to cook and stir until thick. Add butter, salt, and baking powder; mix well. Then add hot mixture slowly to beaten eggs, stirring constantly. Pour into greased 2-qt. casserole. Bake in 425 deg. oven 45 minutes or until set. Serve at once in baking dish with plenty of butter. Serves 8.

HOPPIN' JOHN

2 cups blackeyed peas
¼ pound lean salt pork
2 cups cooked rice

salt and pepper to taste
dash of Tabasco

Wash peas and soak overnight. Drain. Add sliced salt pork. Cover with salted water and cook about 40 minutes, or until tender. Some liquid should remain in the pan; if not, add enough to cover bottom of pan. Stir in cooked rice and seasonings. Place over low heat and stir; cover and heat. Serve immediately. Serves 4-6.

PEANUTTY RECIPES

PEANUT BUTTER SAUCE FOR VEGETABLES

1 tablespoon butter or margarine
¼ cup peanut butter
2 teaspoons flour

½ teaspoon salt
pepper
1 cup milk

Melt butter in pan over boiling water. Blend in the peanut butter. Add flour and seasonings and stir until smooth. Stir in milk slowly. Cook over boiling water until thick, stirring constantly. Serve on cooked cabbage, onions or cauliflower. Makes about 1 cup.

BAKED APPLES WITH PEANUT TOPPING

4 medium apples
1/3 cup raisins
½ cup orange juice
½ cup water
2 tablespoons flour
⅛ teaspoon salt

¼ cup sugar
½ teaspoon cinnamon
1 teaspoon grated orange rind
1½ tablespoons butter
1½ tablespoons peanut butter
¼ cup chopped salted peanuts

Core apples without cutting through the blossom end. Pare apples one-third of way down. Put raisins into centers of apples. Place apples in a baking dish and pour orange juice and water around them. Combine flour, salt, sugar, cinnamon, orange rind, butter and peanut butter, mixing until crumbly. Stir in peanuts. Spoon mixture over apples, piling some in a mound on top. Bake at 375 deg. about 1 hour, basting with the liquid every 15 minutes. The top of the filling may be toasted by placing in the broiler the last 5 minutes. Serves 4.

CREAMED CELERY WITH PEANUTS

1½ cups celery cut in 1-inch pieces
¾ cup liquid (cooking liquid plus milk)
1 tablespoon flour
¼ teaspoon salt

pepper
1 tablespoon butter or margarine
¼ grated cheese
¼ cup chopped salted peanuts

Cook celery until tender in small amount of boiling salted water. Drain. Measure cooking liquid and add enough milk to make ¾ cup. Mix flour and part of liquid until smooth. Stir into rest of liquid. Add seasonings and butter; cook slowly until sauce thickens, stirring frequently. Stir celery and cheese into the sauce. As soon as cheese melts, remove from heat. Add peanuts. Serves 4.

PEANUT BUTTER MUFFINS

2 cups sifted flour
3 teaspoons baking powder
1 teaspoon salt
¼ cup sugar

1/3 cup peanut butter
2 eggs, beaten
1 cup milk
2 tablespoons melted fat or oil

Sift dry ingredients together. Work in peanut butter. Combine eggs and milk; pour into dry ingredients. Add fat and stir just enough to moisten dry ingredients. Fill greased muffin pans 2/3 full and bake in 400 deg. oven 25 minutes. Makes 12 large muffins.

INDEX

INDEX (Continued)